Small Hotels & Inns of Eastern Spain

Charming Places to Stay
in Valencia, Murcia and Teruel

Derek Workman

SANTANA BOOKS

Small Hotels and Inns of Eastern Spain
Published by Ediciones Santana S.L.,
Apartado 41,
29650 Mijas Pueblo (Málaga) Spain
Tel: (0034) 952 485 838. Fax: (0034) 952 485 367
info@santanabooks.com

First published in 2006

Design by Chris Fajardo

Cover photograph and Chapter title photographs by Derek Workman

Printed by Gráficas San Pancracio S.L.

Depósito Legal: MA-872/2006
IBSN: 84-89954-51-8

For my sons, Jim and Tom.

There is a Spanish saying that goes:
Have a son, write a book, and plant a tree,
and your name will live forever.

It's time I planted a tree.

ABOUT THE AUTHOR

Derek Workman came to Spain on the cusp of the millennium, having spent his first half century following divergent career paths including Merchant Navy officer, antiques restorer, muralist, exhibition organiser and audio producer – none of which particularly equipped him to be a travel writer. Having researched his first Santana book, **Inland Trips from the Costa Blanca**, he discovered that, not only did few people realise just how lovely is Eastern Spain, very few were aware of the splendid accommodation available, himself included. Hence, **Small Hotels and Inns of Eastern Spain**.

ACKNOWLEDGEMENTS

The indefatigable Miles Roddis, author of so many Lonely Planet guides that I've lost count and who was always there with lunch, a word of wisdom and a glass of stiffener at the "I've had enough of this" point; Guy Hunter-Watts, who guided me through the intricacies of Filemaker Pro software and eased my life by allowing me to use the format that he had so finely tuned in his excellent *Small Hotels and Inns of Andalusia*; Ken Brown, who gave me the opportunity to write the book and who had the foresight to realise that Eastern Spain is far more than just a darn good beach; the many hotel owners who lifted my spirits by the sheer enthusiasm of their endeavours; and, for the future, all those who will keep me up to scratch and make the next edition even bigger and better. Thank you, one and all.

CONTENTS

INTRODUCTION

For the past four decades eastern Spain, and most notably the Costa Blanca, has been thought of as a sun, sea and sand holiday destination, but what many of those sunning themselves on the golden beaches did not know was that within 20 minutes they could be dipping their toes in mountain streams or meandering along narrow roads through stunning mountain scenery with great vistas down to the Mediterranean. And awaiting them a half-hour further are a wine-growing plateau, hill-top castles, gorgeously decorated churches and Disneyesque villages with narrow, cobbled streets so peaceful that little moves except the shadows or a languid cat.

As Spain is said to encompass Europe and Africa, from the lush greenery of Galicia to the arid plains of Andalusia, the same can be said of the Valencian Community, from the pine-covered mountains of the Maestrazgo in the north of Castellón province to the semi-desert in the south of Alicante — a change of continent in a two-hour drive, with the undiscovered regions of Teruel and Murcia a short drive further on.

Until little more than a decade ago few visitors to eastern Spain set foot in the interior, partly because of the lack of decent accommodation. All that has changed, particularly over the past five years, and the region now has top-quality places to suit every need and pocket, from tiny village *casas rurales* to sumptuous hotels, often designed or restored by the owners themselves, incorporating family heirlooms that make you feel part of a Spanish family and not simply a paying guest.

The increase in demand for good-quality accommodation away from the coast has led to the rejuvenation of many old buildings that would once have continued to decay into ruin: mills, mansions, country houses of the once-rich, tiny farms and village houses, all full of history now brought back to life.

Among the unexpected bonuses resulting from the influx of foreign residents is the opportunity for the traveller to experience a wide range of cultures and their different approaches towards entertaining their clientele. The British, German, Dutch, and Scandinavians have opened up hotels and rural dwellings, bringing their national comforts with them to blend with the wonderful Spanish countryside, warmth and way of life. In many cases it is these *extranjeros* that have led the way in opening up the more rural areas.

Equally important: the new breed of hoteliers recognises that their guests want more than simply a comfortable bed and many of the hotels in this book offer a range of activities, from walking to plant identification, cooking to canoeing, wine-tasting to writing. Private spas, relaxation classes, wonderful regional gastronomy made with home-grown ingredients...this side of eastern Spain offers a totally new experience.

USING THIS GUIDE

Hotel numbers

The hotels have been numbered on a north-to-south, west-to-east basis through the Valencia region, beginning with Morella almost at the tip of Castellón and ending in the south of Alicante province. Teruel and Murcia follow. The hotel numbers on the maps correspond to the numbers on the top of the pages giving details of each hotel.

Addresses, email, etc

In almost every case the address that appears in the book is the address of the hotel itself, as distinct from the postal address, which can often be different. The letters "s/n" after the name of a street or road mean *"sin número"*, i.e. without a number. Thus, unless you know exactly where the hotel is, you could struggle to find it without adequate directions which, hopefully, this book provides. Following the instructions in the Getting There section should ensure safe arrival, but most of the hotels have their own web pages which often give more detailed information on their facilities and on how to find them than space in the book allows. Nearly all the hotels use email for booking and this is often the quickest way to check availability or confirm a booking. To call a hotel direct from outside Spain, first dial the Spanish code 0034, which must also be used when dialling a mobile phone (Spanish mobile phone numbers begin with a 6). You will notice the same telephone number for a few *casas rurales* in the Vall de Gallinera and Vall de Laguart. This is a central booking number, but all the houses are privately owned by members of the local cherry-growing cooperative.

Description

Any system, stars or otherwise, used by other organisations has been totally ignored in this book. These are my personal observations and may differ from those of other people's.

Rooms

When booking a room it is always best to specify if you want a room with a double bed *(habitación con cama de matrimonio)* or twin (*habitación con dos camas*) as the Spanish sometimes refer to a room with twin beds as an *habitación doble*. Suite or semi-suite can be anything from a room with enough space for a sofa or a couple of easy chairs to a separate lounge and bedroom. Best to check at the time of booking.

Prices
All prices were confirmed in late 2005. Where a range of prices is shown this can be because of varying room size or because of seasonal differences — allow for the possibility of a price increase but it is unlikely to exceed 10 per cent.

MEALS

Breakfast
Spanish breakfast rarely starts before 9am and is usually little more than toast or a croissant and tea or coffee. So, if you want to leave early, it is best to pay your bill the night before and plan to have breakfast at a café, where you will usually have a much wider selection to choose from. Breakfasts in foreign-owned hotels can vary from a large cold buffet with meats, cheeses and pastries to a full-blown British.

Lunch/Dinner
Prices quoted in the book are generally that for a set lunch (although you will usually have a choice of dishes) or an average for *à la carte*. Some hotels also offer a fixed price menu. If you would like the set menu ask if they have one (*¿hay un menú del dia?*). If you would like to dine *á la carte* ask for *la carta*. *Menú* usually only refers to the fixed price menu, except when a *menú degustación* is offered. This is a sampling menu and often a good way to try the regional cuisine.

Directions
The space in the book for describing how to find any given hotel is limited, so it is always best to take a decent, reasonably large-scale map with you. Many web pages have detailed information and maps that you can print out.

Disabled Access
Disabled access in Spain is rarely as good as in northern Europe,

but they are getting there. Where we say that a hotel is accessible for disabled visitors it means that at the very least a disabled person can access their room and bathroom but wheelchair-users and more severely disabled people may need assistance. It is always best to check with the individual hotels prior to booking as to the exact facilities they provide.

USEFUL HOTEL INFORMATION

Registration
You are required by Spanish law to register on arrival at a hotel, for which you will need your passport or I.D. The receptionist will sometimes suggest they complete the registration while you install yourself in your room, but it is best to wait until the registration is completed and retrieve you passport in case you forget it the following day.

Language
Many people come to Spain assuming that everyone speaks English, an idea they are soon disabused of when they step outside the main tourist towns on the coast. Trying to get a message across to a receptionist by speaking in a loud voice will not succeed; patience and politeness will. The Spanish are a very amenable race and will do their utmost to help, but a few words of their language, no matter how pidgin-ish, will go a long way.

Booking/credit cards
Many hotels and some casas rurales now ask for a credit card number and deposit when making a booking. This can vary (although it should be made clear at the time) and is usually non-refundable. This is done because of the number of no-shows that hotels get, especially at weekends.

Arrival and departure times
You will sometimes be asked to give an approximate arrival time and, if you think you are going to be late, it is always worthwhile calling the hotel to let them know. Some have a policy of holding rooms until a certain time, but most are flexible so long as they know you are definitely going to arrive. It is always worth checking at what time you have to vacate. Most

hotels will be happy to look after your luggage if check-out time is earlier thanyou would like to leave.

Heating
Visitors to Spain are often surprised that in winter months it can get pretty cold, especially in the mountains. Most hotels have heating, even if they don't have air conditioning, but it is wise to come prepared. That image of sipping a glass of wine on a terrace can soon pall if you forgot to bring a sweater for cool late autumn evenings.

Noise
Spain is the second noisiest country in the world, the first being Japan. It will soon become apparent that the Spanish like a boisterous chat with their friends into the small hours, so even at a country hotel the noise could well go on until way beyond what you might be used to. If you are a light sleeper, ask for a quiet room when you make your booking, but don't be embarrassed about asking to be moved if the noise is too much for you.

Our criteria for including places
Deciding what constitutes a good place to stay is highly subjective, but I hope that my experience of staying in the good, bad and doubtful has given me enough of an idea about what will appeal to the traveller.

On their forays abroad some people like to experience a totally different culture, and there are plenty of places to stay in this book that are as Spanish as Spanish can be. Others like a bit of home comfort and for those I've included a number of places that are unreservedly British, even down to afternoon tea and a good British fry-up. And there are plenty of places in between.

I've tried to include hotels and B&Bs to suit as wide a range of tastes and pockets as possible. If your favourite isn't here, this is no reflection on how it is run or the people who run it. Certain areas have far more places to stay in than others and, to some extent, this will dictate a hotel's or *casa rural's* inclusion. It's a lot easier to find somewhere pleasant to stay in Alicante province than it is in Castellón for the simple reason that tourism is far more advanced in the former than in the latter. But, even if the accommodation in Castellón may be marginally more basic, it is such a stunningly beautiful area that it would be a shame not to go there because it is short on hotels offering jacuzzis. No hotel has been included in this book that I would not be happy to stay at myself.

Your opinions and recommendations

If you have a special place you recommend to friends or discover somewhere in your travels that you think worthy of including in the book, please let me know. This also applies to any hotels and B&Bs in the book that might not come up to expectations. This information will help us improve subsequent editions. Any information you can give about your dining experiences at the hotels or interesting places to visit will also be gratefully received.

EXPLANATION OF SYMBOLS

 Owners/staff speak English

 Hotel has room(s) with disabled facilities

 Bedrooms have air-conditioning

 Hotel has its own swimming pool

 Pets are accepted, regardless of size

 Vegetarian food can be prepared

 Credit Cards are accepted

 Good walks close to the hotel

 Garden/patio area where guests can sit outside

 Hotel is suitable/caters for young children

 Hotel has its own car park

MAPS OF EASTERN SPAIN

MAP 01

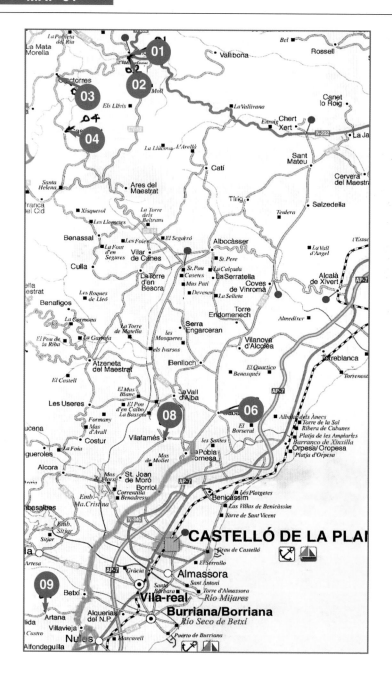

MAP 02

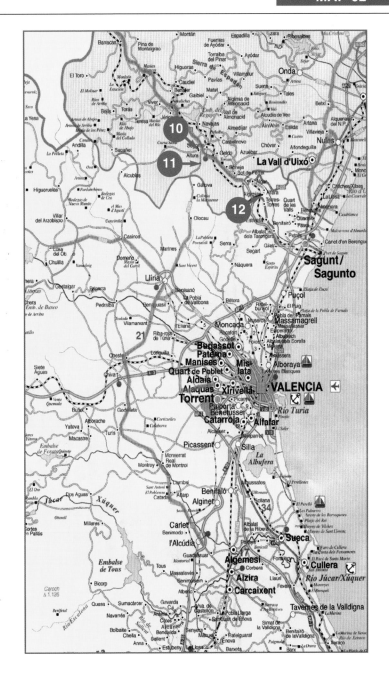

MAP 03

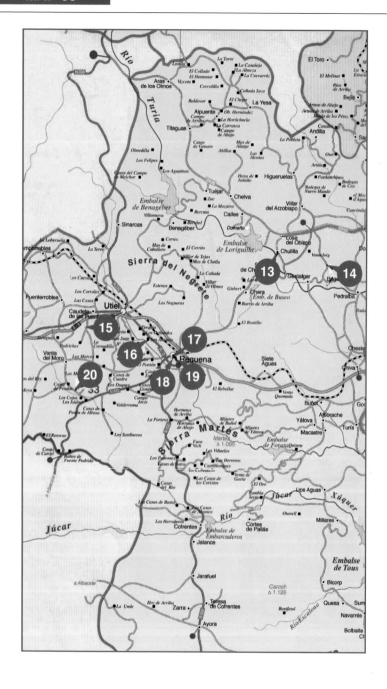

MAP 04

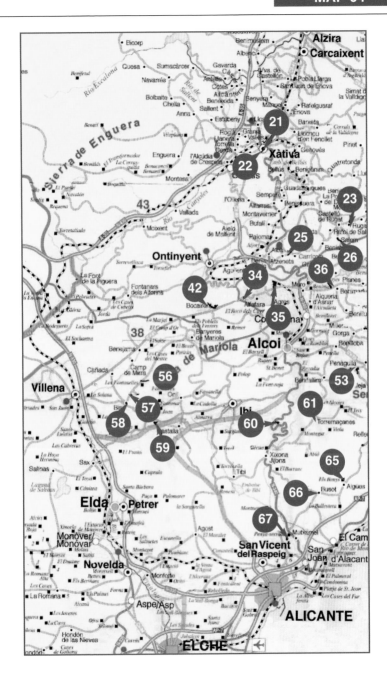

MAP 05

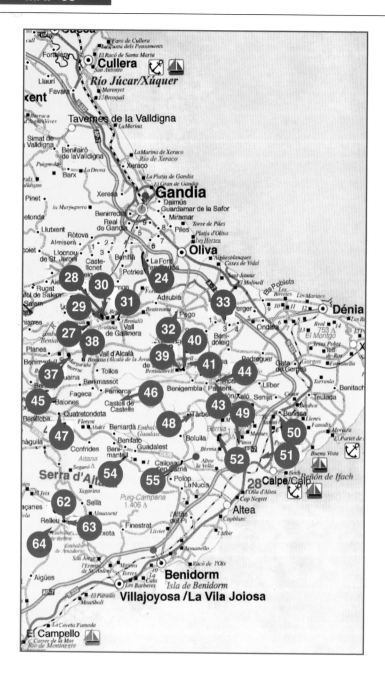

MAP 06

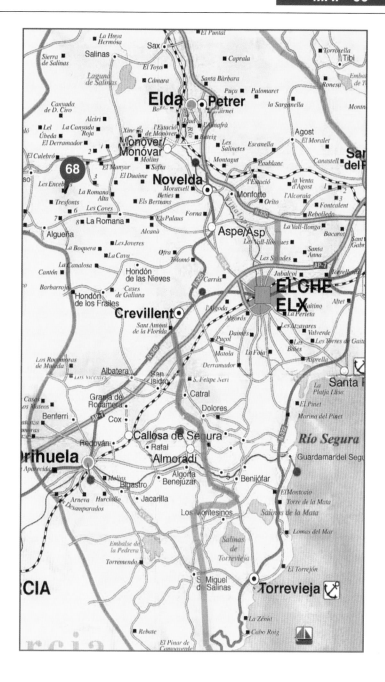

MAP 07

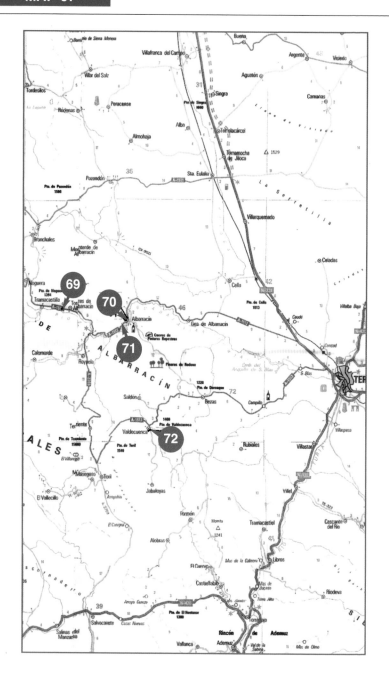

MAP 08

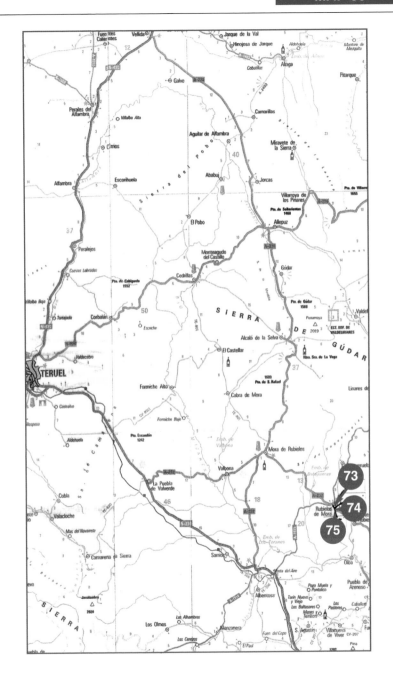

MAP 09

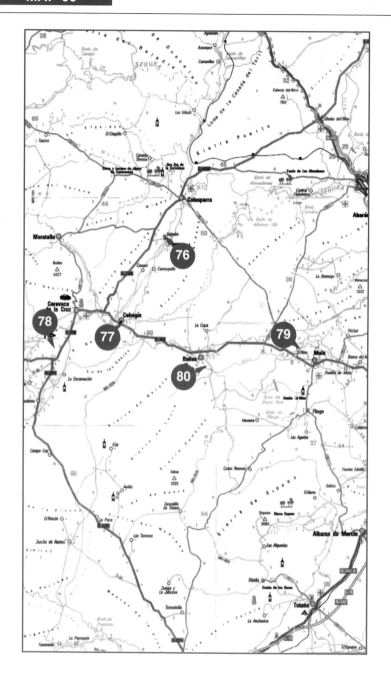

HOTEL REVIEWS BY PROVINCE

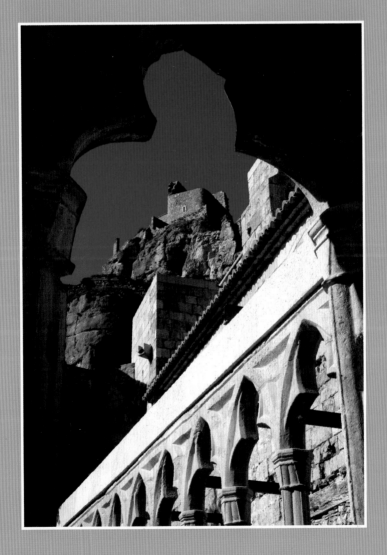

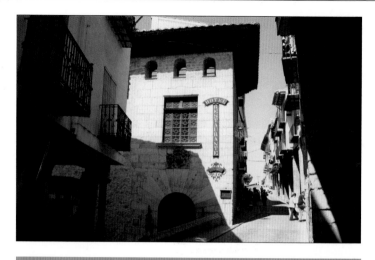

HOTEL CARDINAL RAM

MAP 01

Cuesta Suñer 1, Morella
12300, Castellón

Tel: 964 173 085 **Fax:** 964 173 218

e-mail: hotelcardenalram@ctv.es

Web Page: www.cardenalram.com

Closed: Never

Bedrooms: 1 Single, 4 Doubles, 12 Twins, 2 Suites

Prices: Single €45, Double/Twin €70, Suite €75 excluding VAT and breakfast

Meals: Breakfast €6, Lunch/Dinner fixed menu €15 including wine, excluding VAT. Vegetarian food if ordered in advance.

Getting there: From Vinarós at the northern coastal tip of Castellón province take the N232 to Morella. As you climb the hill to the city look for the sign for the Porta San Miguel. Entrance to the walled city must cleared by the hotel. Telephone or walk to the hotel first so that they can inform the gate-keepers. Phone numbers are on the entrance kiosk. Go through the gate, take the left after the tourist office, continue to a Y-junction and take the right, upward, fork. You will see the hotel before you as you pass between stone colonades about 200 metres further.

Management: Jaume Peñarroya Carbó

It is almost impossible to mention Morella and not include the Cardinal Ram in the same sentence. As you walk up the ancient, colonnaded main street, there it is right in front of you, a 15th-century palace standing four-square as the centre of Morella life since Papa Luna, the infamous anti-pope from Peñiscola popped in to meet the King of Aragón in 1444. A beautiful mural in the entrance hall tells the story, and the stunning stone, arched stairway is equally impressive. Today's architects, with all their computer technology, would be hard pushed to equal it. All the rooms are furnished in keeping with the grandeur of the *palacio*; the parquet flooring and heavy antique furniture glow. Bright bedcovers and rugs of local design and manufacture add vivid splashes of colour. In a major renovation in 2005 all the bathrooms were completely refitted and residents can luxuriate in a hydro-massage shower. If you take one of the suites, you'll gaze through windows that Papa Luna himself might well have looked out of five centuries ago. The restaurant wins praise for its regional gastronomy, including the highly prized truffle, a speciality of the area.

What to see and do: Morella walled city (a National Heritage site), mountain villages of Forcall, Mirambell and Cantiviejo, mountain walks.

HOTEL EL PASTOR

MAP 01

Calle San Julián 12, Morella
12300, Castellón

Tel: 964 161 016 **Fax:** 964 173 322

e-mail: info@hoteldelpastor.com

Web Page: www.hoteldelpastor.com

Closed: Never

Bedrooms: 4 Doubles, 7 Twins, 1 Triple

Prices: Double/Twin €62 (single occupancy €46.50) Triple €76.50 including breakfast but excluding VAT

Meals: The hotel does not have its own restaurant but the same family own El Meson del Pastor a two-minute walk away. Plenty of excellent restaurants and tapas bars in the city

Getting there: From Vinarós at the northern coastal tip of Castellón province take the N232 to Morella. As you climb the hill to the city look for the sign for the Porta San Miguel. Entrance to the walled city must cleared by the hotel. Telephone or walk to the hotel first so that they can inform the gate-keepers. Phone numbers are on the entrance kiosk. Go through the gate, take the left after the tourist office, continue to a Y-junction and take the left, downward fork. The hotel is on the left at 200 metres. You can unload and return to park the car outside the city walls.

Management: Mercedes Gasuella Bareda

From the stone façade of the Pastor you would never believe that a few years back the site was a pile of rubble, the remains of two old houses. Everything is new and of excellent quality, from the foundations upwards. Pretty stencilling on the walls leads the eye upwards towards delightfully decorated bedrooms, each with its own colour scheme and all furnished in grand style, with glowing reproductions of local furniture styles and brightly coloured bedspreads in the Morella style of weaving. (It's worth taking one home — you can buy them at very reasonable prices at shops nearby.) If you don't mind the climb to the gods, ask for room 302. It is a double with its own terrace and spectacular views across mottled red Mediterranean roof tiles to a landscape of rolling green hills. Morella has superb local gastronomy, most notably the truffle and *cecina*, a beef version of *jamón serrano*. One of the best places to sample the local food is the Mesón del Pastor, a couple of minutes away. The historic walled city is an excellent centre for exploring the beautiful mountainous region of the Maestrazgo.

What to see and do: The walled city, Mirambel village, Santuario Virgen de la Balma.

HOTEL EL FAIXERO

MAP 01

Carretera Iglesuela 7, Cinctorres
12318, Castellón

Tel: 964 181 975

e-mail: www.elfaixero.com

Closed: Never

Bedrooms: 3 Twins, 6 Doubles, 3 Triple

Prices: Double/Twin €50 + VAT 7% (€25 single use), Triple €60

Meals: Breakfast included, week day lunch menu €8.50, Dinner €5-20.
Vegetarian food if ordered in advance

Getting there: From the coastal A7 motorway take the CV10 from
junction 47 in the direction of Borriol and Pobla Tornesa, just after which
take the left to Vall d'Alba (CV15). Stay on this road until just after
the turning for Ares del Maestre and the junction with the CV12 to
Morella. Continue in the direction of Vilafranca del Cid to the CV124,
signposted Castellfort. Continue through this village into Cinctorres. El
Faixero is on the left.

Management: Joaquín Deusdat and Inmaculada Molinos

In an area not over supplied with country hotels, El Faixero comes as a special delight, with its handsome Modernisme (Art Nouveau) façade and tree-shaded patio. The name comes from the *fajas,* long tasselled scarves woven on the looms once present in almost every village house. The *faixero* was the person who would collect the cloth and walk many kilometres to sell it, his call "El Faixero! El Faixero!" ringing through the narrow streets to tell everyone to bring out their wares as he was off on another trip. The hotel retains its links with the textile past as early last century it was the grand home of one of the local factory owners. Much of the original decoration remains, including some of the wooden ceilings, and the use of modern building materials in the restaurant, which housed what was the factory, adds to the impression of a well-designed hotel. Inmaculada, with 25 years' experience running a family restaurant in the village, is in charge of the kitchens, which specialise in local dishes, hearty meats and cheeses.

What to see and do: Morella historic walled town, village museum, marked paths.

CASA FOLCH

MAP 01

Calle Major 4, Castellfort
12159, Castellón

Tel: 964 445 700

Closed: Never

Bedrooms: 2 Double, 4 Twin, 2 en-suite

Prices: Double/Twin €40-46 including VAT

Meals: Breakfast included, dinner to order €10

Getting there: From the coastal A7 motorway take the CV10 from junction 47 in the direction of Borriol and Pobla Tornesa, after which take the left to Vall d'Alba (CV15). Stay on this road until shortly after the turning for Ares del Maestre and the junction with the CV12 to Morella. Continue towards Vilafranca del Cid to the CV124, signposted Castellfort. Casa Folch is on the left-hand side as you leave the village, almost opposite the church.

Management: Manuel Folch Tronchón

Driving through the Maestrazgo, an area running from northern Castellón into Teruel province, offers an image as far removed as you can possibly get from tourist Spain. Kilometre after kilometre of twisting country roads with nothing to break the sublime view other than the occasional farm or village perched on a hilltop. Castellfort is a typical village of the region, little more than a cluster of houses gathered around a church for safe-keeping, and Casa Folch is a typical village house, tall and narrow, built to keep the summer heat and winter cold outside the stout wooden front door. It opened its doors early in 2005 to cater for those discovering the natural beauty and tranquillity of this area. Simply but comfortably furnished, it is a place for those who love quietness and long mountain walks. The gastronomy of the Maestrazgo is based on good meat and cheese and it is one of the main areas in Spain for truffles. Simple regional dishes can be provided at Casa Folch, but they must be pre-ordered.

What to see and do: The walled town of Morella, plenty of marked paths.

CASA ANNA

MAP 01

Plaça la Font 5, Chodos/Xodos
12134, Castellón

Tel: 964 370 157

e-mail: www.hotelrural-casaanna.com

Closed: Monday

Bedrooms: 1 Single, 5 Doubles, 4 Twins

Prices: Single €22, Double/Twin €60-70 including VAT

Meals: Breakfast €4, Menu del dia €10, Lunch/Dinner a la carte €20 including wine and VAT

Getting there: From Castellón follow the CV16 to l'Alcora and then the CV165 to Azeneta del Maestrat. From her take the CV171 to Chodos. The hotel/cafe is in the corner of the main square.

Management: Anna Gonell

Some maps will tell you that the road ends in Chodos. They're wrong — a narrow country road takes you onward into Teruel. But, even if Chodos was the end of the road, it's worth the trip to Anna's door if you love wide-open spaces, glorious vistas and good country cooking. Anna's grandmother ran a small hotel in the same premises decades ago, although you wonder who her clients were in such a tiny village miles from anywhere. In 2002, the family restored the house to create a *casa rural*, and a splendid job they made of it. The comfortable bedrooms are furnished in a pleasingly modern rustic style, and the spacious lounge has a big open fire – it can get pretty cold in them thar hills in winter – but it is the views that make this small family-run hotel so memorable. At weekends the restaurant is full of people gorging on meats cooked on the big wood-burning grill that fills one side. December to February is truffle season — the area is famous for them — but at any time of the year you should try the local grilled meats rubbed with truffles.

What to see and do: This is walking country and best enjoyed solely for that.

HOTEL L'ALDABA

MAP 01

Calle La Fira 1, Cabanes
12180, Castellón

Tel: 964 432 180 **Fax:** 964 431 934

e-mail: info@hotelaldaba.com

Web Page: www.hotelaldaba.com

Closed: 10-21 January, 6-17 September

Bedrooms: 2 Doubles, 3 Twins

Prices: Single €57, Double €75-99

Meals: Breakfast €7.50, Guest menu lunch and Dinner €20

Getting there: From the E15 coastal motorway take exit 46 and follow the signs for Borriol and Poble Tornesa and then to Cabanes. Follow the signs into the village and, just after a small garden on the right with a palm and a stone arch, turn left. The hotel is on the corner.

Management: Mari Carmen Albero and Javier Tomás

Originally the old coaching house for the village, L'Aldaba has been brought into the 21st century with an elegance and an Edwardian style that brings to mind an Agatha Christie novel. You almost expect Hercule Poirot to walk through the door, twirling his waxed moustache. The salon is delightful, with soft sofas to sink into in front of an open fire, exposed stone walls and original beams, and long floral drapes. The whole ambience is of a comfortable country house, but in this case set in the centre of a small village a short drive from the sea. As much of the original house as possible has been preserved and the young owners, Javier Tomás and his wife María Carmen (Maica) Albero, won a well-deserved award for the design of L'Aldaba shortly after it opened in December, 2004. Each of the individually designed bedrooms are comfortable if not spacious, with burnished dark wood furnishings and immaculate white linen. A couple of them have pretty little private terraces. The two-fork restaurant, reopening in April, 2006, after being extended, serves typical Valencia cuisine. It features dishes like *conejo con caracoles* (rabbit with snails) and *cabrito lechal horneado* (oven-baked kid's leg), with a few of chef Maica's original ideas.

What to see and do: The salt-water spa at Oropesa, Desierto de las Palmas, Vilafamés historic village.

MAS DE MADALENA

MAP 01

Carretera CV190 Km 22, Lucena del Cid
12120,Castellón

Tel: 96 476 0282 / 630 558 934

Web Page: www.masdemadalena.com

Closed: Never

Bedrooms: 4 Suites

Prices: €60 plus 7% VAT

Meals: Breakfast included, Lunch/Dinner €25 plus VAT (must be booked in advance)

Getting there: Take the CV16 from junction 47 (Castellón) on the A7 coastal motorway in the direction of L'Alcora, then the CV190 for Lucena del Cid. From there continue on this road for 4.5 kilometres in the direction of Castillo de Villamalefa. Just after a sign for Venta Marieta at the top of a rise, take the left, following the signs for Mas de Madalena. Ignore the Granja Mas de Madalena and stay on the road until it arrives in the car park of the hotel.

Management: Pablo Aguilar

There can't be many hotels where you can have a wonderful night's rest in rustic silence, enjoy a rich gastronomic experience, and — should the fancy take you — get married, baptised or christen your child. You can at Mas de Madalena, in a beautiful tiny chapel, one of the special features that brings people to this lovely hotel set at the foot of the Penyagolosa mountains. Even without the ecclesiastical opportunities, Mas de Madalena is a delightful spot in its own right. The four independent suites are themed in rich colours, blue, red, green and garnet. Antiques fill the rooms and, if you're in the mood for a touch of decadence, choose the blue room with its splendid four-poster bed and deep sofas. If you have a child with you, they can feel equally luxurious in their own bedroom with its daintily painted 19th-century bed. The gardens are designed for strolling. If you feel like a bit of company without conversation, snuggle up to the old tramp — he may be a sculpture but has a friendly smile. You'll be smiling too after dinner of, for example, *paella de bogavante* (lobster) or caramelised peppers over toasted goat's cheese, rewarding the palate with a wine from the hotel's excellent *bodega*.

What to see and do: Torre Ibérica nature area, ceramic museum at L'Alcora, spa and hot water springs of Montanejos.

EL JARDÍN VERTICAL

MAP 01

Calle Nou 15, Vilafamés
12192, Castellón

Tel: 964 329 938 / 677 472 396 **Fax:** 964 329 939

e-mail: casarural@eljardinvertical.com

Web Page: www.eljardinvertical.com

Closed: Never

Bedrooms: 4 Doubles, 2 Twins, 1 Suite

Prices: Double/Twin €100-120, Suite €150 excluding VAT and breakfast

Meals: Breakfast €12, Lunch/Dinner €25-30 excluding wine

Getting there: Leave at junction 47 on the A7 motorway, following the signs for Sant Joan de Moró and Vilafamés. When you come to the village follow the signs uphill for the *Casco Urbano* and *Ayuntamiento*. When you reach the square in front of the town hall, take the narrow street in the far right corner. You can unload in front of the hotel and they will direct you to parking

Management: Gloria Diaz-Varela

From the moment you ring the bell at El Jardín Vertical you are in for a surprise. When you step inside, you enter what seems like an enclosed courtyard with a beautiful floor laid in a complex pattern of rounded beach stones. A sinuous stairway glimpsed through a beautiful doorway leads to the sumptuous bedrooms and comfortable lounges. Gloria left Madrid and her work as an interior designer to completely restore the nobleman's house that had lain derelict for decades. Where possible, she has conserved the original structure and fittings of the house. But, calling on her years of decorating the homes of Madrid, she has given it new life with wonderful rich, earth colours, glowingly exposed stone walls, original beams and artful touches. The restaurant serves food any five-star hotel would be proud of. It's a delight to take an *aperitivo* on the terrace overlooking the orange and olive groves spreading almost as far as the eye can see. Vilafamés is one of those Spanish villages that postcard producers search for, with its tumbling cobbled streets and flower-bedecked walls.

What to see and do: The historic village, Museo de Art Contemporaneo, the castle's prehistoric paintings.

CASA DE LA COSTERA

MAP 01

Calle San Vicente 28, Artana
12527, Castellón

Tel: 964 611 243

e-mail: casadelacostera@eresmas.com

Closed: Never

Bedrooms: 4 Twins

Prices: €55-67 including VAT and breakfast

Meals: €9 to order

Getting there: Take junction 49 on the A7 coastal motorway for Vall D'Uixó, following the signs for Villavieja and Artana. As you enter Artana, going in the direction of Eslida, take the right opposite Tallers Silvestre into Carrer Ample. First left into Calle Constitución and when you arrive at Plaça Nova take the left at the top of the square into Calle Calvario, a bumpy road between garages. Follow the signs at the top for La Costera.

Management: Teresa Blasco

Enter La Costera by the front door and it looks like a typical tiny village house. Your impression changes as you walk into the lounge, even more so as you climb the tiled staircase to the second-floor living room, and then step on to the patio and see the swimming pool and delightful gardens. Cleverly placed trees make you think that the Calvario, the stations of the cross en route to a hilltop shrine, and the castle are all part of your private playground. Rooms are simple but there is so much room in the house and gardens that you need never feel short of privacy. Teresa has designed her rural hotel so that you really don't want to leave. Breakfast on the patio, lunch around the pool and dinner in the antique-filled dining room all tempt you to stay on. With luck a room with private terrace will be vacant, offering you views over the village rooftops to the Sierra Espadà National Park. Disabled people can enjoy a walk around the village on a route designed as part of the *Cruz Roja Itinerario Adaptado* scheme.

What to see and do: Caves of the Vall D'Uixo, Museum of Natural Sciences at Onda and the Peñas Aragonese.

HOSPEDERÍA EL PALEN

MAP 02

Calle Franco Ricart 9, Segorbe
12400, Castellón

Tel: 964 710 740 **Fax:** 964 712 410

e-mail: hostalpalen@hotmail.com

Web Page: www.segorbe.com

Closed: Never

Bedrooms: 1 Single, 1 Double, 6 Twins

Prices: Single €45, Double/Twin €62

Meals: Lunch/Dinner a la carte approx €20. Restaurant closed Tuesdays but there are plenty good places to eat in Segorbe

Getting there: Leave the N234 Sagunto-Teruel road at km 27. At roundabout with two exits for Segorbe take the first. Shortly after passing under a blue metal railway bridge follow the sign pointing left for the Tourist Office. Take the next right and park in front of the Tourist Office (behind the Town Hall). Walk to the front of the Town Hall and take the narrow street opposite, turning left at the end

Management: Florencia Sales Bolumar

You can imagine Florencio's family saying: "Your collections or us!" One could imagine the main reason he opened his restaurant, hotel and bar was to have space to display his finds. And what a collection! You can barely climb the stairs without knocking into ancient ceramic jugs and bowls. Beautiful antique washstands clutter the landings and racks of walking sticks, display cases of miniatures, ancient grind stones, Roman artefacts, 16th-century hand-painted tiles, hand-carved dolls houses (the list goes on and on) fill every vacant space or hang on bright yellow-painted walls. You take breakfast on the terrace, shaded by a stout olive tree in a tub, listening to the chirruping of canaries in chi-chi Victorian cages. You will undoubtedly be overwhelmed by Florencio's collection, but make sure to take lunch in the restaurant in the basement. Not only are the dishes very good, mainly based on grilled meats, but the walls are lined with enough historical armaments to outfit an army.

What to see and do: Historic old town, Segorbe cathedral, Cueva Santa, the strange underground sanctuary at Altura.

MASÍA FERRER

MAP 02

Partida Ferrer s/n, Segorbe
12400, Castellón

Tel: 607 473 844 **Fax:** 607 473 845

e-mail: gerente@masiaferrer.com

Web Page: www.masiaferrer.com

Closed: Never

Bedrooms: 6 Doubles, 5 Twins, 15 with bunk beds sleeping 4

Prices: Double/Twin €56 including breakfast

Meals: Lunch/Dinner guest price €12 excluding drinks

Getting there: Leave the N234 Sagunto-Teruel road at the junction for Geldo/Segorbe. Go left, under the road bridge, and at the third roundabout (including the one at the exit) follow the sign Camino de Cabrera on the small country road (there's also a sign for Masía Ferrer). Stay on this road for 7 km, when it ends in front of the masía.

Management: Victor and José Luis Martínez Juan

The road to Mas Ferrer dips through fields and pine forests until you eventually see the great *masía* in front of you with nary a neighbour in sight. Welcome to tranquillity. The building looks as if it has been weathered for centuries but, while the sterling stone façade is historic, the interior rose from the ground in 2004. Vicente and his brother, José Luis, haven't just created a rural retreat bathed in almost complete silence, they are in making a self-sustaining hotel and restaurant which will also offer courses to future generations of eco-students. The kitchen uses salads and vegetables from their gardens and fruit comes from their own trees. Farmyard hens give eggs and the herd of goats wandering their land provide the excellent, hand-made *queso de cabra* and sometimes delicious roast kid's leg, a speciality of rural Spain. In a few years their own vineyards will provide the wines to accompany their excellent menu, a tradition dating back to the 14th century when the estate provided wine for the monastery at Altura. Everything is grown organically. Rooms are furnished in chunky Mexican pine and have views that seem to go on forever.

What to see and do: Segorbe historic centre, walks in the natural park Sierra Caldera, follow the route of the masías to see these old farmhouses.

VALENCIA PROVINCE

EL SECANET

MAP 02

Calle Torres Torres 25, Algímia d'Alfara
46148, Valencia

Tel: 962 626 527

e-mail: info@elsecanet.com

Web Page: www.elsecanet.com

Closed: Never

Bedrooms: 2 Doubles

Prices: €60 & €70

Meals: Dinner on request €18-20

Getting there: Take the N234 Sagunto-Teruel road, exiting at km 14 for
Algímia d'Alfara. You enter the village park beside the fountain opposite
the sharp left-hand bend (there's an avenue of trees beside the turning).
Calle Torres Torres is the street behind the fountain

Management: Gemma Compañ Compañ

When the village barber died, Gemma and her husband Salva bought his house to make sure no undesirables moved in next door to their home. Not wanting it to stand empty, they have created one of the most delightful stays in the Valencia region. Only a half-hour drive from Valencia city centre and 15 minutes from the beach at Sagunto, El Secanet is a world away from city bustle, sitting in a quiet street in an equally quiet *pueblo*. It boasts long vistas over orange groves to distant mountains known as *Les Mamelletes* ("the breasts" in *valenciano*). With only two bedrooms, one of them almost a suite, it's almost like staying in your own rented cottage. Except that it probably wouldn't have a glorious raised swimming pool, oodles of lounge areas, great big gardens shared with the family, and a collection of rare hens, ducks, and peacocks. Gemma is a delight: no rush, no stress and, if you want breakfast at 11, it's your holiday. A total and utter delight.

What to see and do: Discover the delights of Valencia city; explore Sagunto Roman castle; and take an underground boat trip in las Cuevas de San José

CASA SERENA

MAP 03

Calle Turia 39, Chulilla
46167,Valencia

Tel: 961 657 083 / 696 832 445

e-mail: lacasaserenaturismo@msn.com

Web Page: www.casaruralserenachulilla.com

Closed: Never

Bedrooms: 1 Single, 2 Doubles, 2 Twins

Prices: Single €40, Double/Twin €43 including VAT and breakfast

Meals: No meals are provided but there is a good selection of *tapa* bars and restaurants in the village. Clients have free use of a well-equipped kitchen

Getting there: Take the CV35 from Valencia in the direction of Rincón de Adamuz. Just after km 48 mark take the CV395 for Chulilla, going through Venacloig. When you arrive at Chulilla take the small road to the left, just after a closed filling station. Park in the small parking area at the bottom of the hill. You will see the sign for the house on the left.

Management: Richard Scott and Peta Szabo

From the sun-filled terrace of Casa Serena you can look down the fertile valley formed by the River Turia, where a steep canyon attracts climbers from all over Europe. You can bathe in the Charco Azul (Blue Pond) or take a picnic to the foot of one of the area's spectacular waterfalls. Chulilla is everyone's idea of a Spanish mountain village, with its houses staggering down the hillside under the watchful eye of the castle, and Casa Serena is everyone's idea of a cosy *casa rural*. Richard and Peta were lucky enough not to have to do any structural work when they bought the house in 2002, but they definitely made their mark in the decoration, with personal items culled from Richard's trips to the East. Bright and colourful (apart from the Black and White room, a single room that is virtually a double), the house exudes "welcome". If you want a bit of exercise, there's a games room with a table tennis table and, if you don't, a cosy lounge with an open fire where love birds Lily and Laska will twitter away to keep you company.

What to see and do: Walk through the canyon to bathe in the Charco Azul, visit the sugared almond-makers in Casinos, in September streets in the village compete to make the most beautiful cross out of recycled material.

CASA CORTINA

MAP 03

Ptda. Campillo de Bugarra, Camino de las Cloches s/n, Bugarra 46165,Valencia

Tel: 962 133 003 / 606 049 328

e-mail: casa_cortina@hotmail.com

Web Page: www.casacortina.es.vg

Closed: Never

Bedrooms: 3 en suite Twins, 4 Apartments with 1 or 2 bedrooms

Prices: Twin €65, Apartments €65-120 including VAT and breakfast

Meals: Lunch €8, Dinner €18-22, both including wine

Getting there: From Valencia take the CV35 Lliria/Rincón de Adamuz road. Shortly after Casinos, at the km 47 marker, turn left for Bugarra. There is a sign for the hotel, 4 km away. Follow signs to left of the road.

Management: Ramón Moreno Castro

Built as a farmhouse during the 17th and 18th centuries, Casa Cortina has been completely, but sympathetically, restored. You enter the central courtyard through a pair of grand wooden doors that formerly graced a convent entrance. To the right is the hotel, with its three en-suite bathrooms and long, narrow restaurant. Opposite this, the stable block has been converted into four small apartments, each with its own bathroom and fireplace. With hardly a building in sight, the farmhouse is surrounded by orange groves and orchards of almonds and peaches. You can wander peacefully on foot or by bike, but if you want a special experience take an outing in a pony and trap. Casa Cortina is slowly expanding to add to its clients' leisure and pleasure. The children's playground will soon be joined by a swimming pool and the kitchen, which specialises in regional cuisine, will be supplied with seasonal vegetables from the farmhouse garden. Nearby Casinos is the sugared almond capital of Spain, where you can sample almost any sweet made from almonds, including *turrón*, the famous Christmas treat, from a number of small, family-owned manufacturers.

What to see and do: The sugared almond makers of Casinos, the meandering hilltop village of Chulilla, have a day out in Valencia city or at its beaches.

HOTEL RURAL ENTRE VIÑAS

MAP 03

Finca del Renegado s/n,
Ctra de Los Isidros km 14, Caudete de las Fuentes
46315,Valencia

Tel: 962 174 029 **Fax:** 962 171 432

e-mail: avensport@avensport.com

Web Page: www.entrevinas.com

Closed: Christmas & New Year

Bedrooms: 1 Double, 11 Twins, 2 Apartments

Prices: Double/Twin €54-70 (single usage €32-57), Apartment €90-125 excluding breakfast and VAT

Meals: Breakfast €6. Lunch and dinner not provided but no shortage of excellent restaurants within a short drive of the hotel

Getting there: A3 Madrid motorway from Valencia to Utiel. N111 to Caudete de las Fuentes and then VV8108 to Los Isidros. Just after sign for Los Pedriches is a small sign for *'Alojamiento Rural'*. Entrance a few metres further on.

Management: Fernando Gómez

As all the promotional material for the Requena region will tell you, a trip to the area is not complete without a visit to a vineyard and *bodega*. If you want to actually stay in one, Entre Viñas, as its name suggests, is right in the middle of a working vineyard, with thousands of hectares of vines laid out in serried ranks around you. The fact that Entre Viñas won an award as the best *casa rural* in the Valencia Community in 2004 must say something, and you can see why when you step through the tall entrance gate that surrounds the hotel's walled courtyard. The 150-year-old building was totally refurbished in 2001. Each of the luxuriously spacious rooms is decorated and furnished in a different style and named after one of the plots of land near the house. Breakfast on the terrace overlooking the vineyard is a splendid way to start the day and deep sofas in the dark peach-tinted living room act like a magnet after a day's sightseeing. The hotel is linked with Avensport, which offers a wide range of outdoor activities.

What to see and do: Signposted walking routes, the historic centre of Requena, local *bodegas*.

CASA DOÑA ANITA

MAP 03

Calle Mayor, San Antonio de Requena
46390, Valencia

Tel: 962 320 737 / 656 341 988 **Fax:** 962 321 110

e-mail: casadeanita@tubal.net

Web Page: www.tubal.net

Closed: Never

Bedrooms: 5 Doubles, 3 Twins (all en suite)

Prices: €54 excluding breakfast and VAT

Meals: Breakfast €6

Getting there: Take the A3 motorway from Valencia and the exit for San Antonio, just after Requena. Shortly after you enter the village on the N111 (in the direction of Utiel) Calle Mayor is on the right. There is parking space in the square in front of the hotel.

Management: Ana Carla Cobo del Prado and Antonio García

Casa Doña Anita began life as the village school in the early 1900s before becoming the family home of Ana's forebears. Little has changed in the interior, which is a splendidly cosy museum of the Modernisme style (a variant of Art Nouveau). When Ana and Antonio decided to restore the building to its original glory before opening as a hotel in 1999, they had copies made of all the original items that were missing, but you'd never tell a replica from the original. Step through the stout, wooden front door and multi-coloured art nouveau tiles, curlicued bentwood furniture and glowing floribunda lamps welcome you. As you climb the stairs to the grand bedrooms, some with the original deep baths to soak in, the walls are decorated in original, hand-painted designs of fans from the 1900s. If you can bother to drag yourself away from the deep, comfortable beds, the tiny cobbled patio is just the place to rid yourself of traveller's fatigue. Antonio's encyclopaedic knowledge of the local wine will direct you to all the best spots for sampling.

What to see and do: Tour the local award-winning bodegas to sample the excellent Utiel-Requena wines, meander the narrow alleys of Requena old town or visit the Parque Geológico at Chelva.

ALOJAMIENTO TURÍSTICO DE LA VILLA

MAP 03

Calle Cristo 21, Requena
46340, Valencia

Tel: 962 300 374

Closed: Never

Bedrooms: 6 Doubles, 3 Twins

Prices: Double €45, Twin €52, single occupancy €32, excluding breakfast

Meals: Breakfast €4, Lunch/Dinner €15

Getting there: A3 Madrid motorway from Valencia. Take first Requena exit and follow signs for old quarter and Tourism Office. Take the slope up between the Tourism Office and castle keep, crossing the plaza at the top. Fourth right (in front of a stunning church entrance) brings you to a plaza with the hotel in front of you.

Management: Maribel López Piqueras

Any guide books that mention Requena invariably tell you that no visit is complete without wandering the narrow alleyways of the old town where generations of Moors, Christians and Jews lived together, in many cases not very happily. Right in the centre, just around the corner from where the Inquisition had its local headquarters, is the home and hotel business of Maribel López. Jovial, chatty Maribel was born and bred in the old quarter and opened her tiny hotel in 2001. The cosy bedrooms are like those you might remember from your granny's: cast-iron and wooden bedsteads with deep, comfy mattresses covered in patterned bed covers, marble-topped washstands and mahogany-framed mirrors, but unlike at granny's each room has a well-equipped en-suite bathroom and TV. Breakfast is taken in the family restaurant below, where you can also sample excellent regional dishes for lunch or dinner. Take a look at the cave that has its entrance from the bar. Much of the old town is built over a warren of caves that have been used for everything from storing oil to bones.

What to see and do: Explore the historic centre of Requena, take walking routes in the surrounding countryside, sample local wines and sausages, both with their own *Denominación de Origen*.

HOTEL LA VILLA (REQUENA)

MAP 03

Plaza de Albonoz, Requena
46340,Valencia

Tel: 962 301 275 / 962 300 374 **Fax:** 962 301 275

e-mail: info@hotellavillarestaurante.com

Web Page: www.hotellavillarestaurante.com

Closed: Never

Bedrooms: 3 Singles, 15 Doubles, 2 Suites

Prices: Single €36, Double €50, Twin €55, Suite €70

Meals: Breakfast €4, daily menu €9

Getting there: A3 Madrid motorway from Valencia. Take first Requena exit and follow signs for *Casco Antiguo* and Tourism Office. Go up the slope between the Tourism Office and castle keep, crossing the plaza at the top. Fourth right (in front of a stunning church entrance) brings you into a plaza with the hotel across to your right.

Management: Maribel López Piqueras

In September 2005 Maribel López opened the doors of her family home opposite the pension she had been running for years in the main square in La Villa, Requena's old town. Her family home was big enough to make a 20-bedroom hotel, complete with restaurant and reception rooms, although it didn't have the lift when she was born and brought up in it. The house – almost a small *palacio* – has been in the García López family for over a century and Maribel has respected as much of the historical structure as possible in the restoration, while offering guests all mod cons. (Book a suite and you get a hydro-massage all to yourself.) In the elegant bedrooms the furniture dates back to granny's days and a fair amount of it has never left the building since it arrived when the family first took up residence. Maribel is immensely proud of her new hotel, but still welcomes visitors in the same chatty way that kept people coming back time and again to her small house across the square, Alojamiento Turístico La Villa, which she still runs for those who want a more homely ambience.

What to see and do: Requena old town, sample the local wines and sausages, both of which have their own *Denominación de Origen*.

HOTEL DOÑA ANITA

MAP 03

Plaza de Albornoz 15, Requena
46340, Valencia

Tel: 96 230 5347 / 656 341 988 **Fax:** 962 323 070

e-mail: casadeanita@tubal.net

Web Page: www.tubal.net

Closed: Never

Bedrooms: 3 Singles, 7 Doubles and 4 Twins

Prices: Single €42, Double/Twin €60 excluding VAT and breakfast

Meals: Breakfast €6, Lunch menu including wine €12 Tue-Fri, Dinner *a la carte* €24-30 excluding wine, including VAT

Getting there: A3 Madrid motorway from Valencia. Take first Requena exit and follow signs for *Casco Antigo* and Tourism Office. Take the slope up between the Tourism Office and castle keep, crossing the plaza at the top. Fourth right (in front of a stunning church entrance) brings you into a plaza with the hotel across to your right.

Management: Ana Carla Cobo del Prado and Antonio García

Antonio proudly shows guests around his new hotel at the drop of a *sombrero*. Tongue-in-cheek, he may try to convince you that it is a 17th–century nobleman's house, but will eventually admit that it is brand new from the ground up, although the massive front entrance arch is pretty ancient. Everything has been made to his own design, apart from the antiques that fill the rooms and the gorgeous, early 19th-century designs for fans that were rescued from a factory closure and decorate the walls along with painted butterflies and birds. Simple murals cunningly disguise the metal lift doors. Every room has either a hydro-massage bath or shower, including the one specifically designed for disabled people with wide doorways to allow for easy access. It is Antonio's proud boast that not a drop of paint was used in the decoration of the building (apart from the murals), all colouring being specially mixed pigments that were blended into the wall finishings. Perhaps not a deciding point for visitors, but it goes to show how much heart went into designing and building the hotel.

What to see and do: Tour the local award-winning *bodegas* to sample the excellent Utiel-Requena wines, meander the narrow alleys of Requena old town or visit the Parque Geológico at Chelva.

CASA DEL PINAR

MAP 03

Ctra. Los Isidro-Venta del Moro km 7, Venta del Moro
46310, Valencia

Tel: 962 139 008 / 609 654 097 **Fax:** 962 139 120

e-mail: diment@wanadoo.es

Web Page: www.casadelpinar.com

Closed: Hotel only closed over Christmas. Open only by prior reservation throughout the year

Bedrooms: 4 Doubles, 2 Twins, 1 Suite, 2 houses sleeping 8/7

Prices: Double/Twin €78, Suite €95 excluding breakfast, houses €900 per week excluding VAT (on application for shorter periods)

Meals: Breakfast €6, Lunch/Dinner €30 excluding wine and VAT

Getting there: From Valencia take A3 motorway to Requena and then N-322 to Albacete. As you leave Los Isidros, take right for Los Cojos and Venta del Moro. Casa del Pinar is two kms from junction on left.

Management: Philip Diment and Ana María Castillo

When Philip and Ana bought Casa del Pinar, a disused winery, in 1989 it was in a semi-ruinous state but they have transformed it into a haven of comfort and gastronomy. You have the feeling that you are in a tiny village; tree-shaded houses surround a central garden with a tinkling fountain and geranium-filled pots abound. A bonus is that this "village" has an enormous swimming pool. Antiques and elegant objets d'art fill the hotel which has spacious, welcoming bedrooms, each with its own large bathroom. The beautifully furnished, self-catering houses are just the way a country home should be, cosy and relaxing, with broad vistas of vineyards and olive groves. Philip's culinary expertise has been recognised by the multitude of awards hanging on the dining-room wall (it's worth inquiring if he's running one of his occasional cookery courses). Ana and Philip welcome you into their home as if you are a friend they haven't seen for a while, and Casa del Pinar draws people back time and time again.

What to see and do: La Vila, historic centre of Requena, Bodega Redondo wine museum in Utiel, sample the wines at the local *bodegas*.

HOTEL MONT SANT

MAP 04

Subida al Castillo s/n, Xàtiva
46800, Valencia

Tel: 962 275 081 **Fax:** 962 281 905

e-mail: mont-sant@mont-sant.com

Web Page: www.mont-sant.com

Closed: 7-20 January

Bedrooms: 3 Singles, 11 Doubles, 2 Twins, 1 Suite

Prices: Single €60-140, Double/Twin €80-160, Suite €320 + 7% VAT

Meals: Breakfast €10, Lunch/Dinner €30

Getting there: From the inland N340 Valencia-Albacete motorway take the exit for Xàtiva. At the time of writing Xàtiva was undergoing considerable roadworks, so follow the signs for the town centre and then the Castillo. The hotel entrance is just after a church on the left.

Management: Javier Andrés Cifre

It would be impossible to write a hotel guide to Eastern Spain without including the Mont Sant, not only because it is one of the most delightful hotels in the region but also because of the ebullience of its owner, Javier Cifre. The hotel, with its salmon-pink washed walls swathed in jasmine, fits in the 15,000 square metres of gardens like a latter-day oasis. Each of the 12 bedrooms is decorated in a different style, often incorporating the antiques gathered by Javier in his student days with iron furniture made in the hotel's own workshops, tucked away behind the wooden cabins in the upper gardens. These cabins, a recent addition to the Hotel Mont Sant, have magnificent views over Xátiva and the valley beyond. Javier's latest project has been to build ramps linking all the garden areas, including the swimming pool and outdoor jacuzzi, making his delightful hotel fully accessible to disabled visitors. The fact that Mercedes and BMW chose Mont Sant to launch their new models in 2005 must say something, as does the fact that an increasing number of couples from the UK are choosing the hotel to plight their troth.

What to see and do: Xàtiva castle and old town, Bocairent old town, remains of Iberian town at Moixent.

HOTEL HUERTO DE LA VÍRGEN DE LAS NIEVES

MAP 04

Avda de la Ribera 6, Xàtiva
46800, Valencia

Tel: 962 287 058   **Fax:** 962 282 177

e-mail: info@huertodelaviergendelasnieves.com

Web Page: www.huertodelaviergendelasnieves.com

Closed: Never

Bedrooms: 2 Doubles, 4 Twins

Prices: Double/Twin €80-120 including breakfast, excluding VAT at 7%

Meals: Lunch €12, residents' Dinner menu €14, both excluding wine

Getting there: From the inland N340 Valencia-Albacete motorway, take the exit for Xàtiva. Follow the signs for the football ground. The hotel is next to it.

Management: Carmen Morales

As you approach the hotel you could be forgiven for thinking you have chosen the wrong place, surrounded as it is by apartment blocks. When you enter, you know you have made exactly the right choice. The house was originally built in the 14th century and though adapted by succeeding generations still retains much of its original form. The entrance hall, with its two grand mirrors and ceramic plaque in honour of the Virgin who gives the hotel its name, leads you from mundane modern life to a curious lounge and bar, where elegant sofas and tables stand on the cobblestones left intact from the original courtyard. Through a pointed arch you get a tempting glimpse of one of the three restaurants, one in a library and another with a tree growing in it. A spiral stairway takes you up to the bedrooms, via a beautiful passageway with enormous windows and 17th-century tapestries hanging on the walls. The six bedrooms are on two floors, each with its own sitting room, the first in well-upholstered "club" style, and the second with a pleasing rustic design set under the roof eaves.

What to see and do: Xàtiva castle, one of the most complete in the Valencian region, the Museo Almudin, and the winding streets of the old town.

LA CASA VIEJA

MAP 04

Calle Horno 4, Rugat
46842, Valencia

Tel: 962 814 013

e-mail: mail@lacasavieja.com

Web Page: www.lacasavieja.com

Closed: 18 December-14 January

Bedrooms: 2 Doubles, 4 Twins and 1 Suite

Prices: Double/Twin €65-86, Suite €130 including breakfast but excluding VAT

Meals: Snack lunches are available on request but the hotel has restaurant open to the public. A la carte €20-30 including wine + VAT

Getting there: From N332 coastal road that skirts Gandia, take the CV60 towards Albaida. After approx 19 km take right on CV691 for Terrateig, Ayelo de Rugat and Rugat. Follow signs for La Casa Vieja through the village. The house is behind the church.

Management: Maris and Maisie Watson de Andrés

Four-and-a-half centuries ago La Casa Vieja was home to the local tax collector, who was required to buy his position from the crown, ensuring that his own home would be a pretty grand place. It was said to be connected to the church and palace by tunnels. Maris will happily point out the details that prove the original owner was someone of substance: the high-arched entry (to allow large carriages access) and the private, interior well. An enormous two-storey inglenook has a cavernous open fire that can be enjoyed from the first-floor open sitting room as well as from the great squashy sofas in the lounge. The house is full of interesting corners, beautifully furnished with antiques, heirlooms of Maris's family. Beds have down duvets and a "pillow menu" (a selection of pillows of different fillings and densities), and each room has individual tea-making facilities, almost unheard of in Spain. A secluded swimming pool almost fills one courtyard while another is used for outdoor dining for the hotel's well-regarded restaurant. Maris is chef and uses the best of local produce, although foreigners and Spanish alike clamour for her sticky toffee pudding. Animals are welcome but incur a seven euros surcharge for room cleaning.

What to see and do: The historic town of Xàtiva and its castle, the mountaintop village of Agres, Albaida's international puppet theatre.

HOTEL MOLI EL CANYISSET

MAP 05

Carretera Font d'en Carròs - Beniarjo s/n, Font d'en Carròs
46717, Valencia

Tel: 962 833 217

e-mail: info@hotelcanyisset.com

Web Page: www.hotelcanyisset.com

Closed: Never

Bedrooms: 7 Doubles, 10 Twins, all en suite

Prices: €100-147 including breakfast +7% VAT

Meals: Guest menu €40 lunch and dinner

Getting there: Bypass Gandia on the N332 and take the exit for Villalonga and Beniarjo. At Beniarjo follow the directions for La Font d'en Carròs and look out for the tall factory chimney on the right, which is part of the hotel.

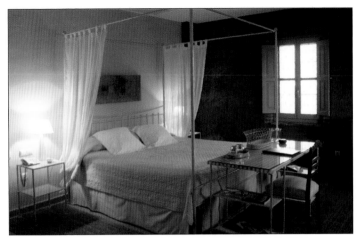

Management: Miguel Cañadas

When Miguel Cañadas began looking for his hotel, it took him two years to find just the right place, a disused and almost derelict rice mill only five kilometres from the beaches of Gandia. It took four years to restore the building – but it was worth the wait. From the outside the hotel looks quite plain. But, when you step through the pale green door, your breath is taken away by the spacious elegance, a glorious mix of antiques, sumptuous modern furnishings and great chunks of machinery that would once have dried and milled the rice but now stand as industrial works of art. The art theme is continued throughout the hotel because the walls are used as an extension of the Rena Bouwen Gallery in Madrid and all the artworks are for sale. Everywhere are neat little visual jokes and hidden corners, but the emphasis is on space, both in the lounge and the sumptuous bedrooms. If you want a little solitude, the pretty library just off the main lounge provides it. La Verenne restaurant on the ground floor is run by Belgians Jenni de Jonge and chef Jo Perpet, who have built up a considerable following for their imaginative cuisine.

What to see and do: The beaches at Gandia, Monasterio de Santa María de Valldigna, picturesque villages of the Vall de Gallinera.

EL PANSAT

MAP 04

Partida Fontavelles s/n, Albaida
46860, Valencia

Tel: 607 167 167

e-mail: info@elpansat.com

Web Page: www.elpansat.com

Closed: Never

Bedrooms: 5 Doubles, 1 Twin, not including breakfast, 8 cabins sleeping 4-8

Prices: Rooms €53.50, cabins €53.50-74.20

Meals: A separately-run restaurant next to the hotel offers a wide range of *tapas* and meals

Getting there: From Xàtiva heading south on the N340, as you pass the sign entering Albaida (just after the Cooperativa Vinícola Virgen del Remedio) you will see the station at a lower level on the right. Take the road immediately opposite (signposted for the hotel) and follow the signs.

Management: Carmen Diana Nacher

The air of El Pansat is never silent; a cockerel crows, pigeons coo and birds chirrup, most of them housed in the complex's aviary. The elegant, bright orange hotel was once a *casa señorial*, home to local big-wigs, whose importance was such that they even had their own private chapel, now deconsecrated but delightfully restored. The vivid colour scheme continues indoors, with a lounge in vermillion and bedrooms in shades of blue. Furnishings are modern rustic. The house is part of a fruit farm that produces peaches, oranges, apricots, plums and olives, and also offers self-contained wood cabins to rent. Energetic guests can use the tennis courts or hire bikes to explore the surrounding area and those of a more tranquil nature can relax in the pine-shaded gardens. El Pansat feels very rural, but is only a few minutes drive from Albaida, a busy little town that is very Spanish. Sights in the old town centre include: the house where the painter José Segrelles spent most of his latter years, an international puppet museum (the only one of its kind in Spain) and the museum of *belenes* (Christmas cribs).

What to see and do: Museums in Albaida, Xàtiva castle and the ancient ice hole at Agres.

GRANJA SAN MIGUEL

MAP 04

Calle Benicadell 19, Salem
46843, Valencia

Tel: 962 883 515 / 696 918 250

e-mail: info@casasanmiguel.com

Web Page: www.casasanmiguel.com

Closed: Never

Bedrooms: 3 Doubles, 2 Twins

Prices: €50-65 including breakfast + 7% VAT

Meals: Fixed menu lunch and dinner €9-13, *a la carte* around €25-35

Getting there: Follow the CV60 to Albaida from the N332 bypassing Gandia. At Castelló de Rutgat take the road to Salem. As you enter the village (just after the sign for the factory shop) a small sign for the Granja San Miguel points to the right. Follow the signs until you drive into the hotels car park.

Management: María Jesús Peiro

Salem would never win a prize for Spain's prettiest village but, as a base to explore the beautiful mountains and picturesque villages surrounding it, the Granja San Miguel is a delightful spot. Originally a working farm, María Jesús took it over when her grandparents retired and put her heart and soul into creating a delightful rustic restaurant before moving on to open her home as a *casa rural*. When you arrive at the hotel the first thing you see are the stables where María houses the thorough-bred horses she breeds, and as you walk through the garden you pass the ducks and hens that provide the eggs for breakfast. There are also a couple of goats and a sheep for the kids to stroke. The house was totally refurbished with the greatest of care and without changing the original structure. Off the central patio is a summer dining room and in the lounge you sit in front of a grand hearth with a hand-painted frieze, surrounded by family antiques and heirlooms. María bursts with enthusiasm for, and justifiable pride in, her house and restaurant. Make sure you try at least one meal in the restaurant to sample excellent regional cooking.

What to see and do: The castle at Xàtiva, beaches of Gandia, or walks in the surrounding sierras.

ALICANTE PROVINCE

CA FERMINET

MAP 05

Calle Pont 11, Benissili
03788, Alicante

Tel: 966 406 700 / 679 831 116

e-mail: info@valterra.org

Closed: Never

Bedrooms: 2 Doubles, 3 Twins

Prices: Double/Twin €60

Meals: No food provided although full cooking facilities available

Getting there: Exit 62 (Ondara) from the A7 motorway, following the signs for Pego (CV700 /C3311) then in the direction of Adsubia/Cocentaina, passing through the Vall de Gallinera. Just as you enter Benisilli a short flight of steps leads to Ca Ferminet. Parking is a few metres further on the left.

Management: Alicia Gregori and Oscar Sergui

The Vall de Gallinera is the cherry valley of the province of Alicante and during February and March a fluffy pink-and-white blanket of blossom covers the hillsides, attracting walkers and artists from throughout the region. Benissili is the topmost and tiniest of the villages of the Vall, where hardly anything stirs except the odd cat. Oscar and Alicia restored this typical village house from the latter years of the 19th century in 2002, opening up the tiny rooms that once stored almonds and carob to bring in light and colour. Warm yellow and cream walls, with the occasional rust red, exposed stonework and a mixture of antique and modern furniture lend the house a comfortable, rustic ambience. In the living room a grand, stone fireplace warms the cockles of winter visitors´ hearts while a tiny, walled patio at the back acts as a sun trap during the summer. Here guests can cook their own barbecue if they don't want to use the well-appointed kitchen to make something grander. Families who rent the two bedrooms on the top floor can use the adjoining kitchen and living room, complete with its own TV, at no extra charge.

What to see and do: Castillo de Benissili, Cova Foradà, walks in the Barranco del Encantada.

CASA RURAL EL CASTELLOT

MAP 05

Calle Raval 9, Alpatró
13788, Alicante

Tel: 966 406 700 / 679 831 116

e-mail: info@valterra.org

Closed: Never

Bedrooms: 3 Doubles, 3 Twins

Prices: €60 excluding breakfast

Meals: Breakfast and dinner can be provided with advanced notice but full kitchen facilities are provided and there are plenty of bars in the village serving *tapas* and lunches

Getting there: Exit 62 (Ondara) from the A7 motorway, following the signs for Pego (CV700 /C3311) then go towards Adsubia/Cocentaina, passing through the Vall de Gallinera. It's very difficult to drive through the village so it's best to park in the small square on Calle San Marco and walk from there.

Management: Ana Pizaro and Juan José Segui

When Ana and Juan José decided to convert Juanjo's grandparents´ house into a *casa rural,* they spent weekends and holidays chipping away at the plasterwork to expose the stone walls and wooden beams beneath — for three years. Their archeological dig unearthed any number of peculiarities, including a ceramic salt pot that had been cemented into the wall, presumably as some sort of hideaway for cash. They left it there and it gave its name to the room: Salteret. (One client even left a tip in it.) The couple's diligence paid off, and a cosy country cottage full of colour, space, comfortable sofas and equally comfy beds is the result of all their hard work. Where pigs and a donkey once ate, guests now dine, in a spacious kitchen/dining room where all facilities are provided free of charge. The top floor has a private terrace and can be booked as a delightful self-contained, two-bedroom apartment at no extra charge added to the room rate. The Vall de Gallinera has some of the loveliest walks in the area and is a favourite for artists who visit during the cherry blossom time of February and March.

What to see and do: Convento de Benisiva, Castillo de Benissili, Almazara de Alpatró (museum of olive oil production).

CASA RURAL LA CARRASCA

MAP 05

Ctra. Alpatró-Benissili s/n, Alpatró
03788, Alicante

Tel: 966 406 700 / 679 831 116

e-mail: infor@valterra.org

Closed: Never

Bedrooms: 3 Doubles, 1 Twin

Prices: €60

Meals: No meals are provided but a well equipped kitchen is available for the use of guests at no extra charge and there are plenty of good restaurants and *tapas* bars in the villages nearby.

Getting there: Exit 62 (Ondara) from the A7 motorway, following the signs for Pego (CV700 /C3311) then towards Adsubia/Cocentaina, passing through the Vall de Gallinera. As you are leaving Alpatró take the right turn signed Benissili. Moments later you cross a small bridge with white bollards, just after the 3 km marker on the CV714. Take the next right up a cemented track and you'll see the house beside the third small track on the right.

Management: Benito Morell Alemany

La Carrasca is everyone's idea of a country cottage: perched on a hill, surrounded by cherry trees and with mountain views as far as the eye can see. This recently refurbished house was originally the family *casita*, a one-roomed agricultural dwelling where the farmers would store their equipment and sleep during harvest time. The front verandah was where wheat from the neighbouring fields was threshed and the ancient well, now safely locked, forms a feature of the dining room. When Benito restored the building, he used as much original and recycled material as possible or tried to copy the original building methods. The two ground-floor bedrooms are enormous, with glowing stone walls, stout beams and exposed cane ceilings. If you visit the valley to see the beautiful cherry blossom during February and March, you can warm yourself in front of a big open fire in the open plan living room/dining room/kitchen. Or, if you fancy a summer fiesta, there's a barbecue on the patio for the ribs and *paella*.

What to see and do: Castillo de Benissili, the freshwater swimming pools of the Barranco de la Encantada, marked walking routes through the mountains.

CASA RURAL LA PARRÁ

MAP 05

Calle San Marcos 9, Alpatró
03788, Alicante

Tel: 966 406 700

e-mail: infor@valterra.org

Closed: Never

Bedrooms: 4 Doubles,1 Twin

Prices: €60 not including breakfast

Meals: No meals available but guests have full use of well-equipped kitchen and there are a numbers of bars in the village that offer *tapas* or lunches, with plenty of good restaurants in the vicinity."

Getting there: Exit 62 (Ondara) from the A7 motorway, following the signs for Pego (CV700 /C3311) then towards Adsubia/Cocentaina, passing through the Vall de Gallinera. It's very difficult to drive through the village so it's best to park in the small square on Calle San Marco and walk from there.

Management: Ramón Morell Alemany

Cherries are the life-blood of the Vall de Gallinera, blanketing the hillsides with blossom in the early months of the year and with deep red fruit at harvest time. La Parrá is one of a group of independent rural dwellings run by the local cherry growers' association. The name comes from the ancient vine that clings to one side of the house, somehow surviving in the stone itself and still producing a regular crop. Ramon restored the house almost single-handedly, using pale colour washes on the walls to enhance the light and open feeling that comes as a surprise when you enter La Parrá. Ask for the blue bedroom on the first floor from which you step through French windows on to your own spacious balcony that overlooks the quiet street below. If that's taken, you can still use the balcony at the top of the house with views over the village and the mountains beyond. Rustic combines with modern and family heirlooms, and the big pine table in the kitchen is just the place to gather around for a chat and a glass of wine.

What to see and do: Cova de Rhull, walks up the Foradà and Barranco de la Encanta.

CASA GALLINERA

MAP 05

Calle Raval 24, Benissivà
03878, Alicante

Tel: 966 406 790 / 620 852 220 / 696 064 529

e-mail: casagallinera@terra.es

Web Page: www.parelelo40.org/casagallinera

Closed: Never

Bedrooms: 3 Doubles, 2 Twins, 1 Apartment

Prices: Doubles/Twin €75, Apartment €118 including breakfast and VAT

Meals: No meals provided apart from breakfast but there are plenty of good restaurants and *tapas* bars in Benissivà and the surrounding villages

Getting there: A7 motorway to Oliva then the CV 715 to Pego. Take the CV700 in the direction of Planes.

Management: Javier Alpuente Oron

Javier's career as an interior designer hits you full-on as you step into the hallway of Casa Gallinera. Deep rich colours and furnishings, rooms full of antiques and ancient farm implements, Asian artefacts and delicate fabrics...everything combines to create a haven of decadent restfulness. Walk through the arch of the tranquil courtyard at the back of the house and you find a big swimming pool with views across the village and the mountains. If you fancy a stroll, you need go no further than the 10,000 square metres of olive, almond and carob trees that are part of the hotel's private garden. Javier and his partner, Pascual, select their own fruit and vegetables to make their breakfast jams and relishes, and they use their own olive oil. If you are lucky, you might arrive on a day that Javier makes some bread in the original *horno de pan*, which could include onions, garlic or olives. You'll probably have just as good a time chatting with the ever-relaxed Javier and Pascual about the delights of the Vall de Gallinera as actually visiting the sites themselves.

What to see and do: Bathe in the natural pools of the Barranco Encantado, go underground at the Cova de Rhull or visit Adzubieta, a ruined Moorish village.

CASA LOUISE

MAP 05

Ptda Michanes, Pego
03780, Alicante

Tel: 965 571 756

e-mail: casalouise@hotmail.com

Web Page: www.casa-louise.co.uk

Closed: Never

Bedrooms: 2 Doubles, 1 Twin

Prices: €45 including VAT

Meals: Full English breakfast included. No other meals provided but there are plenty of restaurants and bars serving *tapas* in the immediate area

Getting there: From N-332 coastal road at Oliva take CV700 to Pego.

Management: Len and Shirley Welford

After 20 years in the pub business in the UK, Len and Shirley decided that the quiet life didn't suit them when they retired to Spain so they opened their house as a B&B. With only three rooms to let the house is almost never empty, not just because of its very British cosiness but because of the extras that the couple offer their guests. These include: an outdoor jacuzzi that bubbles all year around, as well as a swimming pool; a barbecue and fully-fitted outdoor kitchen for visitors who don't want to leave the gardens surrounded by orange groves; a small television lounge for anyone who doesn't want to miss the box, although most people prefer to gather around the table on the shady terrace to chat. A big English breakfast starts the day and, although Len and Shirley don't provide lunch or evening meals, they can recommend plenty of good local restaurants as well as interesting places to visit. Pego is only a 15-minute drive from the beaches of the north Costa Blanca, but is also ideally placed to discover the mountain villages of Alicante province.

What to see and do: El Vergel Safari Park, mountains villages of Vall de Gallinera, Historic centres of Dénia and Jávea.

PUEBLO JARDÍN

MAP 05

Calle Muestra Consuelo Sanchis 7, Benimeli
03769, Alicante

Tel: 965 587 127 / 667 919 585

e-mail: contact@puerblojardin.com

Web Page: www.pueblojardin.com

Closed: Never

Bedrooms: 2 Doubles, 2 Twins, some En suites

Prices: Double €50-60, Twin €45-50, minimum 2 nights stay or there is a €5 surcharge per room for single night usage

Meals: Dinner on request €12-20

Getting there: From A7 coastal motorway take exit 62 for Ondara. In Ondara turn left and follow the CV731 in the direction of Beniarbeig. After 1.5 km turn right for Beniarbeig and left immediately after the blue bridge in the village. When you arrive at Benimeli,take second left (Calle Senyor) up to church and left onto Maestra Consuelo Sanchis.

Management: Valerie Kohler i Cyrille and Yves Cyrille

If you happen to be staying at Pueblo Jardín when air steward Yves isn't away on one of his international flights, you may have a breakfast treat of some of his hand-made delicious pastries. If he's not there, Valerie will prepare you one of her splendid dinners, a mixture of French, Moroccan and Indian cuisines with a flamboyant touch of her own. They are dab hands in the kitchen, both having chefs as fathers, and Valerie's mother has one of the best restaurants on the Costa Blanca — she'll make you a special reservation. The décor owes much to their international travels, but within the historic context of a Valencia village house, albeit a pretty wealthy one. Note the gorgeous, original tiled floors and in the entrance hall the initials BL for Berard Llul, the original owner. The themed rooms will transport you to India, Morocco, Provence and various points east. With almost as many *salons* as bedrooms, guests don't have to share one another's company, though everyone will want to dine on the palm-shaded patio. The couple are one of the new breed of *casa rural*-owners, with enough experience of sleeping in other people's houses to know how to provide comfort in their own.

What to see and do: The beaches and castle of Dénia, 15 minutes drive away; Benidoleig caves; bodegas and Saturday antiques market at Jalón museum, Font Roja National Park.

CASA RURAL EL PINET

MAP 04

Masia El Pinet s/n, Alfafara
03838, Alicante

Tel: 965 529 039 / 605 960 888 **Fax:** 965 510 141

e-mail: info@elpinet.com

Web Page: www.elpinet.com

Closed: Never

Bedrooms: 2 Doubles, 3 Twins (one can be used as a triple), Apartment sleeping 6

Prices: Double, Twin €65, Triple €75, including breakfast, Apartment €150, all excluding VAT

Meals: Only breakfast provided but Alfafara and Bocairent have some of the best restaurants in the region

Getting there: From San Vicent del Raspeig take the N340 to Alcoi. Stay on the road past Cocentaina until you see the second sign for Muro de Alcoy. Take the slip road and go under the N340 in the direction of Agres. Continue past Agres and through Alfafara for 2km, when you will see a sign for El Pinet on the right. Pass the white house on the left and the El Pinet is the next building.

Management: Sergio Castelló

The original farmhouse on the estate was built in the 18th century, but its present appearance suggests that someone with a rather mixed bag of architectural ideas couldn't resist playing with the façade, with its crenellations and Modernista (Catalan version of Art Nouveau) details. The overall effect, though, is delightful, the sort of mini-country castle you'd love to park the vintage Rolls in front of. El Pinet is split into two. One part, the original porter's lodge, is the *casa rural* with rooms rented individually, and the other, once the home of the coachman, an apartment that sleeps six. Whatever the exterior might be trying to say, the interior is decidedly rustic. The furniture looks as though it has been there forever, which it probably has because the house was the summer home of Sergio's grandparents, but the result is one of rural cosiness. Lawns surround the sinuously shaped swimming pool and, for a quiet read on a summer's day, there are lots of sitting areas under the tall pines that give the house its name. The large internal patio is just the place for breakfast when the weather is at its best.

What to see and do: Bocairent medieval village, blanket-making factories of the area, Agres.

MASÍA DE SAN JOAQUÍN

MAP 04

Carretera Muro-Agres Km 8, Agres
03870, Alicante

Tel: 629 937 571

Web Page: www.casaruralagres.com

Closed: Never

Bedrooms: 1 Single, 5 Doubles, 5 Rooms with 2-3 beds

Prices: €25-35 per person per night, excluding breakfast and VAT

Meals: Breakfast €3. Some of the region's best restaurants are within a short drive of the house

Getting there: Take the N340 from San Vicent del Raspeig to Alcoi. Stay on the road past Cocentaina until you see the second sign for Muro de Alcoy. Take the slip road and go under the N340 in the direction of Agres. At 6 km from Muro you will see a sign on the right for a cement road that leads to the masía's car park.

Management: Asunción Calaguig

Lovers of Edwardiana need look no further than the Masía de San Joaquín.
Its furnishings are in that style, all bought brand new by Asunción's
grandparents, although the house itself goes back much further, to the
end of the 18th-century. The décor is otherwise eclectic in a family
inheritance style. The *masía* (farmhouse) consists of two, independent
houses, the original, where the wealthy owners lived during the summer
months, and a second, originally barns, storerooms and accommodation
for the labourers who worked the one million square metres of the estate.
The houses are let either complete or by the room and, if you would like
to do your own cooking, a fully-fitted kitchen is at your disposal. You
may want to because the *masía* has its own smallholding, from which
you can buy ecologically grown vegetables as the season dictates. You
can also help the local farmers pick such crops as almonds, asparagus,
hazelnuts, mushrooms and pears. Asunción is the fifth generation
Calabuig to own San Joaquín and the history of the family is portrayed
on the walls in paintings and photos.

What to see and do: Agres village and the snow cave, the Palacio Comtal
at Cocentaina, medieval, high-rise village of Bocairent.

HOSTERÍA ELS BANYS

MAP 04

Balneario s/n, Benimarfull,
03827, Alicante

Tel: 965 530 177 / 659 535 726

e-mail: elsbanys@hotmail.com

Closed: Never

Bedrooms: 7 Doubles, 3 Twins

Prices: €60, single occupation €40, including breakfast, excluding VAT

Meals: Only breakfast provided but plenty of restaurants and *tapas* bars in nearby Muro de Alcoy

Getting there: From San Vicent del Raspeig take the N340 to Alcoi. Stay on the road past Cocentaina until you see the second sign for Muro de Alcoy. Take the slip road and go straight through Muro. After a long bridge the twisting road begins to climb. You reach a 90-degree bend 2.5km from Muro with a copse on the left. Take the rough track on the left immediately after the bend. Though not signposted, this leads directly to the Hostería's car park. If you see a large red house on your left seconds after the bend, you have gone too far.

Management: Maria Carmen and Águeda Torre Grosse

Plenty of small hotels have been converted from large family homes once the children flew the coop, but there must be few which have become a family home and then changed back again. Such is the case with Els Banys, a delightful house that was originally built in 1846 as a spa, making the most of the high sulphur content in the water running through the grounds. Many years after it closed, during the Civil War, María Carmen and her husband bought the building to use as a family home, but with only two children the 12-bedroom house took some looking after. It became a hotel in 2004, but for all that it feels as if you are staying in a comfortable family home, and indeed the family still live here. The decorative style, as María Carmen says, incorporates something of everything, but is wonderfully welcoming and cosy. A large covered patio provides welcome shade on summer days and there is plenty of garden space to take an evening stroll. You can even sample the spa water from the original spring, and in the dining room are a couple of the original baths carved from solidblocks of marble and stone.

What to see and do: The Moorish village of Bocairent, Agres and its snow cave, Alcoi Moors and Christians museum.

CASA RURAL EL CHATO CHICO

MAP 05

Plaza de la Iglesia 6, Beniaya
03788, Alicante

Tel: 965 514 451 **Fax:** 965 514 161

e-mail: enquire@elchatochico.com

Web Page: www.elchatochico.com

Closed: Never

Bedrooms: 2 Doubles, 4 Twins

Prices: €48-66 (single usage €30-39) including breakfast and VAT

Meals: Dinner to order €20

Getting there: Leave the N332 coast road at Olive, heading for Pego and thence in the direction of Vall de Ebo and Sagra. Just out of Pego a steep road to the right directs you to Vall de Ebo. Continue on this road until you pass through Alcalà de la Jovada. A couple of kilometres further a country road signposted Beniaya goes to the left. You arrive at the village square. El Chato Chico is right beside the church.

Management: Paul Walmersley and Jakkie Spenser

When Jakkie and Paul found their *casa rural*, it was "a ruin with a stream running through it". The origins of the building are said to go back over a thousand years, when it was once the home of a Moorish holy man, but now it is a delightful, cosy hideaway. With its exposed stonework, deep chairs and sofas to doze in after a day's walking, a TV lounge for those who like the box and a library for those who don't, El Chato Chico is an oasis of tranquillity, which comes as no surprise in a village with only 14 permanent residents. Jakkie provides good, wholesome dinners if you order them in advance and Paul will give you all the help you need for local walks if you give him a couple of days' notice. The mountains surrounding Beniaya are a joy to walk in for either a stiff hike or gentle stroll. In centuries past it was one of the most important centres for gathering wild herbs in the whole of Europe, and thyme, sage and rosemary perfume the air as you meander the mountain paths. After more than 30 years in Spain, there's not much hat Jakkie doesn't know about the area's nooks and crannies that don't appear in the guidebooks.

What to see and do: The ancient caves of the Cova de Rhull, the ruined Moorish village of Adzubieta and the ancient *nevara* (ice house).

CASA RURAL LA CASOTA

MAP 05

Camino Viejo entre Fleix y Campell s/n, Fleix, Vall de Laguart
03791, Alicante

Tel: 965 583 646

e-mail: info@lacasota.com

Web Page: www.lacasota.com

Closed: Never

Bedrooms: 3 Doubles, 1 Twin, 1 Suite, 1 Two-bedroom self-contained house that sleeps 6

Prices: Double/Twin €60, Suite €80, House €140 excluding VAT and breakfast

Meals: Breakfast €6, Dinner €16.50 excluding wine

Getting there: From Exit 62 on the A7 coastal motorway take the road to Ondara then the CV725 for Orba. From Orba take the road to the Vall de Laguart, passing through Campell. Just as you enter Fleix, take the small road on left and follow this until you see the hotel entrance on a bend.

Management: Joaquina Garrido

Driving through the gates of La Casota is like driving into a tiny village, complete with higgledy-piggledy cobbled footpaths, tinkling fountain, fruit-laden trees and Pancho the dog to welcome you. Following close behind will be a smiling Joaquina, known to everyone as Quini. Once used for the storage and drying of grapes to make the raisins, the buildings were abandoned in 1905 and lay empty for almost a century until Quini and her husband took over the massive restoration project that transformed La Casota into one of the most delightful *casas rurales* in the Valencia region. Some of the tastefully decorated en-suite bedrooms lead directly out into the gardens, while others have small private terraces. Warmly-lit, comfortable lounges and a cosy dining-room are furnished with antiques. Eggs from La Casota's own chickens are served at breakfast, and fresh organic fruit and veg from the gardens are used with skill by Quini in her excellently inventive cooking. Two beautiful Palomino ponies are at guests' disposal and Pancho will happily have a wander through the hills with you for a bit of company.

What to see and do: Marked walking routes through mountains, Neolithic rock paintings at Pla de Petracos, Barranco del Infierno. museum, Font Roja National Park.

CASA RURAL TERRANOVA

MAP 05

Ptdo. Terranova 6, Fleix, Vall de Laguart
03791, Alicante

Tel: 966 406 700 / 670 831 116

e-mail: info@valterra.org

Closed: Never

Bedrooms: 1 Single, 2 Doubles

Prices: Double €60 including VAT

Meals: No meals available but full cooking facilites provided. There are some excellent restaurants and *tapas* bars in the surrounding villages

Getting there: From Exit 62 on the A7 coastal motorway take the road to Ondara then the CV725 for Orba. From Orba take the road to the Vall de Laguart, passing through Campell. Just as you enter Fleix take the small road on the left. The *casa rural* is the beige house on your right almost immediately after the turning.

Management: Victoria García Márquez

The road that twists its way up the Vall de Laguart really is the road to nowhere. Once you get to the top and have savoured the stunning views over the olive groves and mountains to the sparkling Mediterranean 30 kilometres away — and sampled the rich mountain food of the Alahaur restaurant — all you can do is turn around and come back, but you'll be missing a breath of tranquillity if you do. In February and March the mountainsides are cloaked with the down-like pinks and whites of cherry trees in blossom and are a magnet to local artists. Terranova is a cosy little spot tucked under the home of Victoria García and her family but, as the house is built on a hill, this *casa rural* has a large terrace with glorious views down the valley to Denia on the coast. Opened in 2001, Terranova is simply but pleasantly furnished. It is let complete or on a room-only basis. There's a well-furnished modern kitchen for the use of visitors, very useful as the nearest restaurant is a 15-minute drive away at the top of the valley, although simpler food can be had just outside the village.

What to see and do: Saturday antiques fair at Jalón, walking in the Barranco del Infierno, Covas del Rull.

CASA RURAL EL CANTO

MAP 05

Calle de la Plaza 41, Campell, Vall de Laguart
03791, Alicante

Tel: 966 406 700 / 609 831 116

e-mail: info@valterra.org

Closed: Never

Bedrooms: 3 Doubles, 3 Twins

Prices: €60

Meals: Meals not provided but clients can use the well-equiped kitchen

Getting there: From the A7 Coastal motorway take exit 62, following the signs for Benidoleig and Orba. From there follow the signs for the Vall de Laguar (some signs will have a 't' on the end). As the road passes through the village, El Canto is on the left just after the small plaza.

Management: Gerardo and Dora Ballester Torrent

The 300-year-old walls of El Canto have seen generations of the Ballester family, each adapting it slightly to suit their own needs, until a complete renovation was done in 2001 to create this delightful casa rural. Perhaps the most unusual feature is the ground-floor gallery housing a permanent collection of Gerardo's beautiful, carved wooden images, and there are more to be seen decorating the walls throughout the house. All the bedrooms are en-suite and decorated differently, with a mix of antique decorative and modern functional, TV and central heating. Guests have a choice of two lounges, one with a fireplace for cosy winter evenings, and a well-equipped kitchen, which is very handy because restaurants in the Vall de Laguart are a bit thin on the ground. From the sun-trap of a terrace at the top of the house you can look across the rooftops of the village to the twin peaks of the Caballo Verde mountains.

What to see and do: Walk through the Barranco del Infierno, visit the natural springs on the Caballo Verde mountain and the Pantano de Isber museum, Font Roja National Park.

HOTEL L'ESTACIÓ

MAP 05

Parc de L'Estació s/n, Bocairent
46880, Alicante

Tel: 962 350 000 **Fax:** 962 350 030

e-mail: reservas@hotelestacio.com

Web Page: www.hotelestacio.com

Closed: Never

Bedrooms: 1 Single, 6 Doubles, 3 Superiors, 4 Twins, 1 Suite

Prices: Single €74, Double/Twin €81, Superior €83, Suite €131 excluding VAT and breakfast

Meals: Breakfast €9, Weekday Lunch €10, Dinner €24 including wine

Getting there: From Alicante take the N330 autopista in the direction of Madrid. Turn off at Villena onto the CV 81 to Ontinyent. When you reach Bocairent turn right at the roundabout with the 'Statue to the Blanket' in the middle. L'Estació is on the right 100 metres up the incline.

Management: Sebastian and Mats Lodder and Josefina Soifer

As the name suggests, L'Estació was originally the town's railway station before it was converted into a delightful hotel. Dutchman Sebastian and his Argentinian wife, Josefina, took over the hotel in early 2004. Together with Sebastian's cousin, Mats, they have built on its former reputation as one of the best hotel/restaurants in the area. Despite the youthful appearance of the trio, they have a personal and family history of hotel management that shows itself in every element of the hotel. Beautiful antiques sit comfortably with the ultra-modern décor, with personal decorative touches everywhere and, unusual for a country hotel in Spain, there is a bedroom completely adapted for disabled people. A shaded patio is splendid for summer dining and, in an area renowned for its good restaurants, that of L'Estació takes some beating. Sebastian and his chef are always experimenting, using mainly local produce, and it's worth trying their speciality, *ternera de piedra*, top-quality beef cooked on a hot stone at your table. You can visit the beautiful Sierra Mariola with locally organised walking and cycle groups or drift across it in a hot-air balloon (the excursions can be booked through the hotel).

What to see and do: Walks and cycle rides on the Vias Verdes (disused railways lines), Sierra Mariola Natural Park.

L'AGORA, BOCAIRENT

MAP 04

Calle Sor Piedad de la Cruz, Bocairent
46880, Alicante

Tel: 962 355 039 **Fax:** 962 355 058

e-mail: mail@lagorahotel.com

Web Page: www.lagorahotel.com

Closed: Never

Bedrooms: 4 Doubles, 4 Twins

Prices: €75-120 excluding VAT and breakfast

Meals: No meals other than breakfast provided in hotel but there is an associated restaurant next door. Excellent *tapas* bars and restaurants in the town

Getting there: From Alicante take the N330 autopista in the direction of Madrid. Turn off at Villena onto the CV 81 to Ontinyent. When you reach Bocairent turn left at the roundabout with the 'Statue to the Blanket' in the middle and across the bridge, following the signs to the centre of the village. L'Agora is on the right just before the Moorish arch into the old town.

Management: Joaquín Piedra and María José Peidro

L'Agora transports you east without even leaving Spain, with the themed bedrooms beautifully decorated with furnishings from owner Joaquín's world-wide travels. Rich, lacquered furniture from China, beautifully-carved and inlaid designs from Pakistan, plaited-rush beds from Kenya and woven decorations from Thailand. The hotel is housed in a delightful early 20th-century *casa señorial*, a home designed for the local gentry. The house has been in the Piedra family since the first stone was laid, but parts of it were never completely finished until its total restoration in 2004. During the Civil War it was used as a quartermaster's store for the region. Although most furnishings are from the east the elegantly-shaped floral forms blend well with the original *Modernista* (Art Nouveau) features still in place, from the sinuously-panelled doorframes to the finely-etched, coloured glass by way of the beautiful floral motif tiles that now decorate the bar. The historical centre of Bocairent appears to tumble down the hillside and is a wonderfully higgledy-piggledy collection of tiny, twisting alleyways. It has the only bullring in the area hand carved out of solid rock. Once the centre of blanket manufacturing (it even has a statue to the manta), it's the place to pick one up at factory prices.

What to see and do: Moorish caves and bullring in Bocairent, the Sierra Mariola Natural Park and the walks of the Castle Routes.

CASA CARRASCAL

MAP 05

Carrer D'Alt 14, Parcent
03792, Alicante

Tel: 679 043 130

e-mail: info@casacarrascal.com

Web Page: www.casacarrascal.com

Closed: Never

Bedrooms: 2 Doubles, 2 Twins, 1 Suite, 1 Apartment

Prices: Double Twins, Suite €75, Apartments €105, Breakfast and VAT included

Meals: Dinner €19.75 including wine

Getting there: Leave the A-7 coastal road at J63, heading in the direction of Benissa. Shortly after you pass through Benissa take the right for Jalon, going through the town in the direction of Alcalali and Parcent. At the T-junction at Parcent take the right turning towards Orba and take the first right turning into the village itself. Then take the first left up the hill, a tree-lined street called Avenida de la Constitución. Take the 4th turning on the right which is almost at the top of the hill and Carrascal is the dark green house about 30 metres on the left.

Management: Sue and David Eaton

When you meet David in casual mode as he welcomes you to Carrascal you would never believe that in the UK he was a high-flying businessman with a staff of sixty and a multi-million pound turnover. He and Sue (she was in marketing) are part of a new breed of hotel and casa rural owner now setting up shop in Spain; thoroughly professional in what they do and going to almost any lengths to satisfy their visitors requirements - and it shows. The house may seem modest in size but it is grand in style, with the elegantly remodelled interior decked out with chunky rustic furnishings that perfectly complement the style of the 17thcentury townhouse. (When the couple had an 'open house' to celebrate their new venture almost all the village turned up, and it seems that at some time in it's history most of the families had lived there.) The small restaurant has grown in both size and regard since the *casa rural* opened in 2005 and the kitchen continues to provide gastronomical glories under the direction of Savoy-trained chef, Ged. A splendid place to relax, but you also have the possibility of trying out a wide range of sports and leisure activities under professional trainers.

What to see and do: Local *bodegas*, Caves at Benidoleig, 15 minutes from beach.

CASA ROSA

MAP 05

Calle Nou, Alcalalí
03728, Alicante

Tel: 966 482 516 / 626 063 127 **Fax:** 966 482 516 / 626 063 127

e-mail: info@casarosaalcalali.com

Web Page: www.casarosaalcalali.com

Closed: Never

Bedrooms: 1 Single, 3 Doubles, 2 Twins

Prices: Single €48 , Double €62 including breakfast and VAT

Meals: There is no shortage of excellent restaurants and *tapas* bars in Alcalalí

Getting there: At the exit for Benissa on A7 motorway follow the signs for Jalón. Pass through the village in the direction of Alcalalí. When you get there take the left into the village, following the signs for Casa Rosa. Park just beyond the house.

Management: Veronica Company

Alcalalí is a curious village, in a sort of limbo, perched on the edge of the Jalón valley, with its large ex-pat communities, before the roads take you up the Sierra d'Alfaro and into the interior proper. Nonetheless, the village still feels very Spanish and there can be no doubting the nationality of Casa Rosa. Enthusiasm for the client's comfort and enjoyment shines through every detail; hair-dryers, tea and coffee-making facilities, embroidered pillows and towels, and vases of roses in the bedroom might be expected (although not always found) in a hotel but not in a small village house. Casa Rosa was converted from family home to *casa rural* in 2000, keeping as many of the original features as possible, and was furnished in keeping with the period, the turn of the 20th century. A huge fireplace dominates the living-room, but if you stay in the summer months you can enjoy the cool of the plant-filled patio. Alcalalí is a rural wining and dining centre for coastal dwellers and as such there is no shortage of good restaurants in the area.

What to see and do: Visit the *bodegas* and Saturday antiques market at Jalón, the medieval tower and museums of Alcalalí, take the 20-minute drive to the beaches of Calpe.

CASA RURAL SERRELLA

MAP 05

Calle San Jose 1, Balones
03812, Alicante

Tel: 965 511 222

e-mail: casaserrella@terra.es

Web Page: www.quietspain.com

Closed: Never

Bedrooms: 3 Doubles, 1 Twin, 1 Apartment

Prices: Double/Twin €40, Apartment €50 breakfast not included

Meals: Breakfast €3, Dinner €15 on request

Getting there: From either Valencia or Campello take the road to Alcoy (N340). A couple of kilometres south of Alcoy take the road to Benilloba. Just past Benilloba turn left for Gorga. In Gorga turn right for Fageca. Balones is the next village. Enter the village by the second entrance, marked *'Centre Urba'* and park on the right under the trees. Walk into the village, take the first left then left again. Casa Serrella is the big peach-coloured house on the left.

Management: Demelza and Mike Whittock

When Mike and Demelza took on Casa Rural Serrella they had 15 years' experience restoring houses in Spain, Mike doing the structural work and Demelza the décor. The restoration has been done to the highest standard, worthy of a much higher-priced establishment, and between them they have created a delightfully comfortable place to spend a few days. Rooms are decked out with a mixture of antique and modern, and short stairways lead to spacious bedrooms, light and airy with large en-suite bathrooms. Mike made the comfortable beds and attractive bedroom furniture – "honeymoon proof," he says. The neat little one-bedroom apartment has its own terrace, and the walled garden is a splendid place for other guests to relax at any time of the day. Demelza provides good basic cooking on request and, as a lifelong vegetarian, makes sure non-meat eaters get more than just a plate of rice and a few veg. Mike's most recent project was to build a bar in the ancient vaulted basement that used to be the *bodega* when the valley's grapes were pressed here.

What to see and do: Historical centre of Alcoy, 13th-century Moorish palace in Concentaina, walking in Font Roja National Park.

CASA PILAR

MAP 05

Calle San José 2, Castell de Castelles
03793, Alicante

Tel: 965 518 157/609 559 382 **Fax:** 965 518 334

e-mail: casapilar@grupobbva.net

Web Page: www.casapilar.com

Closed: Never

Bedrooms: 3 Doubles, 3 Twins

Prices: €60-70

Meals: Dinner €18 including wine. Needs to be booked

Getting there: From junction 65 of A7 motorway (or from Benidorm) take the C3318 to Callosa d'en Sarrià. From there follow the signs for Bolulla and then Tàrbena. As the road continues to climb after Tàrbena take the first left for Callosa. When you arrive at Callosa turn right and continue into the village centre until you come to Calle San José.

Management: Pilar Vaquer and Juan José Alemany

Only a few decades ago the postman for the village of Castell de Castells also served Callosa d'en Sarrià, which is now a thriving town a short drive inland from the beach at Benidorm. Each day he would walk the 14 kilometres there and back between the two villages to deliver the mail. Pilar now retraces the route from her cosy *casa rural* with a walk linked with the Repos de Viajar in Callosa. She was born and brought up in Casa Pilar, discovering the highways and hidden corners of her region, and lived in the house until she married. Visiting the house is like visiting your granny's, but a granny who is either very fit or has servants because everything glows with a sheen that can only be gained from plenty of elbow grease. As a girl Rosa would definitely not have dined in the current dining room, a basement with domed ceiling and the original mangers where the donkeys feasted. On request Rosa can map out in English walks of three to ten hours. Casa Rosa richly deserves the Q mark, the national tourism award for quality, given to only six *casas rurales* in the Valencia Community.

What to see and do: Neolithic cave paintings a Pla de Petracos, the protected nature area of Los Arcos, the village ethnology museum showing life as it was in Castelles generations ago.

HOTEL RURAL ELS FRARES

MAP 05

Avda. Pais Valencia 20, Quatretondeta
03811, Alicante

Tel: 965 511 234 **Fax:** 965 511 200

e-mail: elsfrares@terra.es

Web Page: www.inn-spain.com

Closed: Never

Bedrooms: 7 Doubles, 8 Twins, 1 Self-catering *casa rural*, sleeps 5

Prices: Double/Twin €80-95 including breakfast plus 7% VAT, *casa rural* €100 per night excluding VAT, min. stay 2 nights

Meals: Breakfast included at hotel, Lunch/Dinner €20-30 including wine

Getting there: On the Benidorm-Alcoy road (CV70), at Benilloba take the Gorga/Millena road. At Gorga take the right to Quatretondeta. Els Frares is on the left as you enter the village.

Management: Brian and Patricia Fagg

Els Frares has been referred by *El Mundo*, a leading national newspaper, as "the icon of rural tourism in the Valencian community". Walkers arrive at the door of Els Frares, either independently or in groups (Waymark Holidays, one of the UK's leading walking holiday companies, has voted the hotel the top European destination). But it's not just energetic hikers who find their way to the cosiness of Els Frares — the roaring fires, deep sofas and comfy beds are a big draw for those who just want to enjoy the peace and tranquillity of the stunning Sierra Serrella. One of the major attractions is Patricia's inventive cooking, an eclectic blend of regional and international, and the restaurant is a favourite with both locals and visitors. Rooms are spacious and airy, light and colourful, each with its own en-suite bathroom. Spanish antiques mix easily with modern furniture in a decorative style that could be described as elegantly rustic. A delightful rural house in the centre of the tiny village, built in the local style, can be rented whole or used as an annex to the hotel. Els Frares was renovated throughout and extended in early 2006.

What to see and do: Visit the historic centre of Cocentaina, stroll through the Font Roja Mariola National Park, study the flora in the micro reserves of the Sierra Serrella.

HOTEL DE TÁRBENA

MAP 05

Calle Santísima Trinidad 1, Tàrbena
03518, Alicante

Tel: 965 884 006 **Fax:** 965 884 231

e-mail: info@hotel-tarbena.com

Web Page: www.hotel-tarbena.com

Closed: Never

Bedrooms: 3 Singles, 3 Doubles/Twins, 2 Suites, 1 Self-contained Studio

Prices: Single €35, Double/Twin €70, Suite €90, including breakfast and VAT, Studio €70 including VAT

Meals: Dinner €14 including wine on request

Getting there: From N-332 coastal road or A7 motorway at Benidorm take the CV70 to Callosa d'en Sarrià, then the CV715 to Tàrbena via Bolulla. Take the narrow street that enters the village and park in the plaza in front of the church. Hotel de Tàrbena is on the street to the right as you enter the plaza.

Management: Francisco Ripoll Molines and Paulette

When the Moors were driven out of Spain towards the end of the 15th century, many mountain villages were left virtually empty. Tàrbena, perched on a hilltop with stunning views to the Med, was one such village. Because of its strategic position, it was re-populated by the Catholic Monarchs, Fernando and Isabel, with islanders from Mallorca. They brought with them their language and family names, examples of which are still found in the village, and the famous Mallorcan sausages, also still found there. Francisco came from the opposite direction, returning from Canada to his home village when he retired. When the children fled the nest, he and Paulette, his French-Canadian wife, converted their lofty village house into a comfortable hotel. To retain the authenticity of the building the couple scoured the demolition yards of Valencia, returning with beautiful doors and woodwork that match the elegance of the modern furnishings in antique French style. The long, slim, en-suite double rooms are virtually suites, except the suites themselves have their own private terraces. Make sure you visit Casa Pinet just around the corner, a self-styled museum-restaurant presided over by the avuncular Jeronimo Pinet.

What to see and do: Fonts de Algar waterfalls and herb gardens, beaches of Benidorm, mountain walks with stunning views.

BLANC CASA

MAP 05

Ptda Marnes 1, Lliber
03729, Alicante

Tel: 965 973 120 /+44 127 36 99352

e-mail: la_blanca_casa@hotmail.com

Web Page: www.blancacasa.com

Closed: Never

Bedrooms: 7 Doubles, 3 Suites

Prices: Double €70, Suite €75-80, incl. full English breakfast & VAT

Meals: Lunches from €6, dinner from €15 including wine. Plenty of restaurants in the Jalón Valley. *Paella* can be brought from local restaurant

Getting there: On the N332 coastal road take the exit for Jalón just south of Benissa. At the T-junction turn right and sharp left (sign for Pinos 7 km). Pass the Restaurant Pinos (8.2km) and after a bridge with blue railings turn sharp right. Stay on this road for 3.5 kms until you see the tall white walls of Blanca Casa.

Management: Steve Callaghan

They shouldn't have told Steve Callaghan that he could not build a mansion-sized villa on top of a mountain. He set out to prove them wrong and, over eight years of construction, the house grew and grew. Even though the villa itself, including turret, is complete, Steve has plans to add tennis courts, stables and Roman baths to the swimming pool and gardens, with their stunning views of the rugged Sierra Bernia and surrounding almond groves. The villa was never intended as a hotel, hence the masses of space in most of the bedrooms. The rooms branch out in two wings from the tower and the entrance hall, with its grand curved stairway and two blackamoors with raised candelabra. The large living room is the venue for musical evenings held around the grand piano, and anyone who wants to enjoy the local cuisine without venturing from the side of the pool can have *paella* delivered to the door from the restaurants down the mountainside. Flippers, li-los and a host of other things are provided for the kids and they even have their own section of the pool. Free kennelling is provided, although owners are expected to feed and exercise their dogs themselves.

What to see and do: Benissa cathedral, Calpe beach, 25 minutes drive, *bodegas* of Jalón Valley.

HOTEL CASES DE SAN JAUME

MAP 05

Ptds Paratella 44, Benissa
03720, Alicante

Tel: 966 499 075 **Fax:** 966 498 208

e-mail: reservas@hotelcasesdesantjaume.com

Web Page: www.casesdesantjaume.co

Closed: 20 Dec-20 Jan

Bedrooms: 3 Doubles, 11 Twins, 12 Semi-suites

Prices: Double/Twin €97-121, Semi-suite €121-144 excluding VAT

Meals: Lunch/Dinner €15-25 including wine but excluding VAT

Getting there: Leave the AP7 coastal motorway at Benissa and head towards the town. Take the third exit on the second roundabout (with the Caprabo supermarket beside it) and continue until you see a sign for the hotel directing you to the left. A few moments later a small sign on the left directs you into the hotel carpark.

Management: María José Tent

At first sight San Jaume looks like a small, one-storey hotel, but when you enter it opens up around you in all directions, following the slope of the hillside. From the great windows of the lounge and reception area with its bright walls and deep sofas, you overlook a patio and swimming pool and begin to realise the full extent of the building. The attractive decoration is in strong colours but does not overwhelm. Placed around the triangle of lawn, the ground-floor rooms' geometric mix of arches, squares and sloped external walls give a curious Aztec village feel. The semi-suites all have small private terraces overlooking olive trees and the country beyond. You could spend the day sunbathing around the huge swimming pool, with a short step to the patio and the modern cafeteria for a snack and a change of vista. If you want a splash in the sea, the beaches are only a few kilometres away. The mainly Mediterranean cuisine of the small, elegant restaurant has an excellent reputation.

What to see and do: 3.5 km from beaches at Benissa, Benissa historical centre, Terra Mitica theme Park.

CASA DEL MACO

MAP 05

Pou Roig 15, Calpe
03720, Alicante

Tel: 965 732 842 / 699 069 926 **Fax:** 965 730 103

e-mail: nacinarcys@hotmail.com

Web Page: www.casadelmaco.com

Closed: All January

Bedrooms: 3 Doubles, 1 Twin

Prices: €66-99 including VAT, excluding breakfast

Meals: Breakfast €9, Lunch €24, Dinner €35 excluding wine, including VAT

Getting there: On the N332 coastal road look for the small sign for the hotel 1.5 km north of Benissa. Follow the signs, which take you directly into the hotel car park.

Management: Barbara de Vooght

Bert de Vooght originally bought Casa del Maco over a quarter of a century ago when he was based in Spain as a photographer. He sold it when he had to return to Belgium but 20 years later he bought it back again, by which time it had become a stylish restaurant. He converted the original family home into a cosy, four-bedroom hotel with each bedroom being given its own style and the restaurant and public rooms fitted out with antiques and stylish modern furnishings. From the lovely dining terrace you look across the great swimming pool to the enormous rock of the Peñon de Ifach nature park at Calpe (the nearest town to the hotel despite the address being Benissa). The size of the hotel means that it is regularly taken over by whole families who treat it as a wonderful holiday villa with a Michelin two-fork restaurant attached. It is also becoming popular with couples coming from the UK to exchange wedding vows under the terrace palms. The Casa del Maco must be one of the few hotels to have its own railway station, where you stick out your hand to stop the local train that shunts up and down the coast between Benidorm and Dénia.

What to see and do: Sierra de Bernia, Guadalest mountain-top village, Peñon de Ifach nature park in Calp.

CASERÍO DEL MIRADOR

MAP 05

Camino les Murtes 13A, Jalón
03727, Alicante

Tel: 607 433 349 or 607 811 197

e-mail: sarah@lesmurtes.com

Web Page: www.villajalon.com

Closed: Never

Bedrooms: 4 Doubles, 3 Twins, 3 Apartments sleeping 2-4

Prices: Double/Twin €100, Apartments €100-200 including breakfast and VAT

Meals: Lunch €8-14, Dinner €18 both including wine and on request

Getting there: Take the CV750 off the N332 coastal road just south of Benissa to Jalón (Xaló). At Jalón take the country road to the left of the Cepsa garage and left at the next T-junction. Turn right where you see a sign for the hotel next to one for a donkey sanctuary and three green rubbish bins just after the 3 km marker. Stay on this road for 4km, when you will see the hotel on the left.

Management: Sarah and Johnny Robinson

The Caserío del Mirado is probably the only hotel in Spain where a teddy bear and box of Lego come as standard in each bedroom. This isn't meant as some form of regression therapy for stressed-out adults (although you can by all means use it for that if you wish) but because, with three children of her own, Poppy, Florence and Charley, Sara Robinson understands keeping the kids happy is halfway to success with the parents as well. When the couple bought the house in 2003, they had it professionally re-styled — an on-going process. But don't get the idea that this is some fancy place for suave young things only; the Caserío is a place were visitors soon mingle and create an informal house party feeling. A beautiful mirador with banquettes bulging with cushions is a glorious place to relax and look down the mountain to the Jalón valley. Or you can lounge around the pool or on the terraces under olive and almond trees. The Caserío is equally popular with those who want somewhere restful after a hard day on the beach or with those more content with a quiet G&T while watching the sun set over the Med.

What to see and do: Jalón *bodegas* and Saturday market, marked footpaths, 30 minutes to beaches at Calpe and Javea.

MAS DE PAU

MAP 04

Ctra Alcoi-Penáguila km 9, Penàguila
03815, Alicante

Tel: 965 513 111 / 965 513 158 **Fax:** 965 513 109

Closed: 24/25 and 31 December

Bedrooms: 8 Doubles, 9 Twins, 4 wood Chalets to sleep 2

Prices: Double/Twin €62, Chalet €69

Meals: Lunch/Dinner approx €25 including wine

Getting there: From Benidorm head towards Guadalest and Confrides on CV70. After passing Confrides, turn off at the sign for Villajoyosa and Alcoleja, just after Ares del Bosc. The road dips and rises quickly. When you get to the top, turn right for Penàguila. Continue through the village until you see Mas de Pau on the hill to the right.

Management: German Martines

As you drive along the winding country road from Penàguila, the Mas de Pau rises from the almond and olive groves of this verdant upland plateau. Reverse the situation and take in the views from the simple but comfortable bedrooms and you are rewarded with glorious vistas of fruit groves filling the valley and climbing the lower reaches of the rugged mountain sides, with pine forests rising above. The original *masía* (*mas* in *valenciano*), the local name for one of the enormous farmhouses you see dotted around the landscape, was built in 1890. It became a hotel just over a century later, in 1993 — see the dates carved into the stout beam that supports the great chimney in the living-room. The hotel is surrounded by walks, but if you prefer less strenuous exercise you can meander the gardens or laze on the enormous terrace surrounding the covered swimming pool whose doors are folded back during summer to let the mountain breezes waft through. If you don't want to be part of the main hotel, there are four Wendy-house-type wooden cabins, each with bathroom, fridge, wood-burning stove and barbecue, set among the Mas de Pau's almond groves.

What to see and do: 19th-century Jardin de Santos, Font Roja natural park, and the Moors and Christians museum in Alcoi.

TORRE ARRIBA

MAP 05

Partida Torre Arriba s/n, Benimantell
03516, Alicante

Tel: 606 770 210

e-mail: torre.de.arriba@wanadoo.es

Web Page: www.torre-de-arriba.de

Closed: 20 December to 7 Jan

Bedrooms: 1 Single, 6 Twins

Prices: Single €39, Twin €78 including breakfast

Meals: Dinner €12 excluding wine

Getting there: Take the CV70 towards Callosa d'en Sarrià from Benidorm. At La Nucia follow the road to Guadalest. After 7 kms you see three restaurants close together, 200 metres further on go left on country road that almost doubles back. Stay on this until it enters the Torre Arriba parking area.

Management: Fritz von Philipp

Hotel guide-writers can easily overdo the word "idiosyncratic", but even that description doesn't do justice to Torre Arriba. A nervous approach up a narrow, winding mountain road ends in a car park, the glorious views from which make the drive worthwhile. When you look at the house it seems just like a pleasant stone cottage, but as you are shown around you can't help breaking into a smile. Everywhere is colour, bright and light, but it's the visual jokes/artworks that make Torre Arriba different from any other pleasant *casa rural*. Squeeze through the narrow door of one bedroom and you see shiny, bright red apples hanging from a bar to form a sort of suspended bedhead. In another a great coil of twigs snakes across the beamed ceiling. In a third, decked out in a nautical theme, star fish (fake) hang over the bed, gently drifting in the breeze. This little heaven on top of a mountain allows you to while away the days in rustic decadence, although there's a gymnasium for those who feel the need.

What to see and do: El Arco Animal Sanctuary and the hilltop old town of Guadalest, 40-minute drive to beaches.

EL REPOS DEL VIATGER

MAP 05

Calle Mayor 4, Callosa d'en Sarrià
03510, Alicante

Tel: 965 882 322/639 902 930

e-mail: jronda@infonegocio.com

Web Page: www.casaruralelreposdelviatger.com

Closed: Never

Bedrooms: 2 Doubles, 2 Twins, 1 Single, all en suite

Prices: Doubles €50-60, Twins €50, Single €36

Meals: Breakfast included and many *tapas* bars and restaurants in the surrounding area

Getting there: From junction 65 of A7 motorway (or from Benidorm) take the C3318 to Callosa d'en Sarrià.

Management: Joaquín Ronda Pérez

Set in the old village square, opposite the 17ᵗʰ-century church, The Traveller´s Rest lives up to its name. What was once the village pharmacy, owned and run by Joaquín's grandfather, now houses one of the best private libraries of local history, flora and fauna in the region. Joaquín will proudly show you the hundreds of historical volumes in the collection begun by his great-great-grandfather. Completely renovated in 2003, the rooms are decorated in soft, warm colours that blend pleasingly with antique furniture, each named to reflect something to do with the family. On the top floor is a small living room and prettily decorated dining room, but in summer months breakfast is taken on the roof terrace, with views over the rooftops to the *León Dormiendo*, the Sleeping Lion, the mountain that sits above Benidorm. Joaquín is a very welcoming chap who is justifiably proud of his hotel and has a fund of information to help you plan your holiday. With Casa Pilar in Castell de Castelles, he has created a walking break with one night in each hotel, the baggage being transported by car while guests ramble the beautiful countryside.

What to see and do: Splash in the pools and fountains of the Fonts d'Algar, visit the mountain-top village of Guadalest or follow the signed paths through the Sierra de Bernia.

MAS FONTENELLES

MAP 04

Ctra Biar-Banyeres km 4, Biar
03410, Alicante

Tel: 686 426 126 / 639 707 924 **Fax:** 965 979 166

e-mail: info@masfontanelles.com

Web Page: www.masfontanelles.com

Closed: Never

Bedrooms: 8 Doubles/Twins, 1 Apartment

Prices: Double/Twin €56-62, Suite €67

Meals: Dinner on request €18

Getting there: As you enter Biar from the direction of Villena and the N330 Alicante-Madrid road you will see a road sign for Banyeres. Leave Biar and the hotel is the white building on the right after four kilometres.

Management: Isabel Aracil Merlateau and Roberto Medoro

There can be few things nearer heaven (at least during the winter months) than sitting before a roaring fire in the Mas Fontenelles lounge and sipping a glass of wine while waiting for one of Roberto's splendid dinners. The house, once the home of Isabel's grandparents, lay in semi-ruin for a decade until the couple decided to turn their backs on the pressures of life in Madrid. It's a great barn of a place with plenty of space. You could almost hold a dance in the bedrooms and the three living rooms allow guests to enjoy privacy. Neatly using the high ceilings to create a sleeping platform above the en-suite bathrooms allows double rooms to be used as family rooms without affecting the pleasing ambience. An eclectic mix of Italian (Roberto) and French/Spanish (Isabel) has ensured a décor that brings together subtlety and style. Paintings by Isabel's mother and from her maternal grandfather's collection grace the rich tones of the walls. In an area known for excellent restaurants, Roberto's inventive mind brings together the best of fresh local produce and inspiration from his Italian roots and world travel. The couple's obvious devotion to their home glows through.

What to see and do: The toy museum at Ibi, Font Roja natural park, Biar's historical centre.

FINCA FANECAES

MAP 04

Ctra de Banyeres s/n, Biar
03410, Alicante

Tel: 902 22 00 52 **Fax:** 965 811 312

e-mail: finca@fanecaes.com

Web Page: www.fanecaes.com

Closed: Never

Bedrooms: 3 Doubles, 11 Twins

Prices: Single €54 Double €66, Twin €66 + 7% VAT

Meals: Lunch approx €20, Dinner €24-30 including wine but excluding VAT

Getting there: As you entre Biar from the direction of Villena and the N330 Alicante-Madrid road you will see a road sign for Banyeres and also a small sign for the Finca. Leave Biar and the hotel is on the left at about one kilometre, signposted.

Management: José Hernández Fanecaes

The small town of Biar is said to have one of the best-preserved 16-18th-century building heritages in the whole of the Valencia region and during Roman times was one of the most important areas for honey in eastern Spain, due to the abundance of flavoursome mountain herbs. Finca Fanecaes stands in 300,000 square metres of almond and olive trees, the latter providing the oil used in the hotel's excellent kitchen. Originally a Moorish farmhouse stood on the same spot, later used to produce oil and wine, but what might at first sight appear to be a fine old farmhouse is almost totally new. It was rebuilt in 2001, although a few of the original walls still remain. The hotel has an air of rustic luxury, featuring highly polished wood and comfortable modern upholstery. As most of the rooms are tucked into the eaves under thick wooden beams, you wake up feeling you are staying in a posh farmhouse. Ask for the suite and your view from the bed will be of Biar castle, illuminated against the night sky. Although Finca Fanecaes has no swimming pool, it is only five minutes´ drive from Hotel Vila de Biar, under the same management, where all the services can be used by Fanecaes residents. Cats and dogs are welcome but must stay in the hotel's kennels.

What to see and do: The whole of the medieval part of the village is virtually a museum, visit the Castle; Ibi toy musuem, Villena's gold find.

LOS DOS TILOS

MAP 04

Calle Barrera 54, Biar
03410, Alicante

Tel: 676 988 836 **Fax:** 965 810 362

e-mail: cataliv@hotmail.com

Web Page: www.losdostilos.com

Closed: Never

Bedrooms: 3 Doubles, 2 Twins

Prices: Double/Twin €50-69 excluding VAT

Meals: Lunch and dinner not provided but there are some excellent restaurants in the town

Getting there: From Alicante take the N330 Madrid road, exit at Villena and head for Biar. Entering Biar, follow the signs for Castalla until you see the tourist office on the left, just before a sharp left-hand bend. Take the left just before the next red-and-white pedestrian crossing, passing to the left of the BBV bank. Right at the T-junction on to Calle Barrera. Next right, following signs for tourist Info. Parking is through the big green metal gates a few metres down this road.

Management: Catalina Vilar

Stepping into Los Dos Tilos is like stepping into a time warp, taking you back to the early years of the 20th-century Modernista period. Catalina was born and brought up in the house and saw no need to change things when she opened it as a small hotel, apart from providing comfortable beds and a cosy atmosphere. One of the major delights of Los Dos Tilos is the garden, enormous for a house in the centre of town. Here are the two *tilos* (lime trees) that give the house its name and whose leaves are used as an infusion. A rose arbour, open-air table tennis, a billiard room and a delightful shaded terrace mean that you barely need to leave the confines of the house. Inside, beautiful examples of locally-made ceramics from years gone by are everywhere and there are lots of corners to just sit and read without bumping into other guests. Nearby Biar castle is one of the most important in the Valencia region and one of only three in Spain with ribbed vaulting. If you can muster even a small amount of Spanish, the guide will give you an excellent tour.

What to see and do: Biar castle, the ethnographic museum and the pottery producing ceramics in local designs.

HOTEL CASETA NOVA

MAP 04

Carretera Vieja Ibi-Castalla km 4.5, Castalla
03540, Alicante

Tel: 666 533 397 / 666 533 391 **Fax:** 966 552 014

Closed: Never

Bedrooms: 6 Doubles, 7 Twins, 1 Suite

Prices: Double/Twin €76, Suite €98 excluding VAT but including breakfast

Meals: Fixed lunch €16, Dinner approx €35 including wine

Getting there: From the A36 that links Alcoy and the Alicante-Madrid N330 above Sax, exit at Ibi and take the road for Villena. After about 3 kms take the small road to the left signed for the hotel. Follow the signs and after about five minutes you will see the deep red-coloured hotel on the right.

Management: Sebastián García Izquierdo

"Baronial" fittingly describes La Caseta Nova, not in the style of some dour Scottish castle but as somewhere done on a grand scale to accommodate grand tastes. In this converted 170-year old *masía*, no expense has been spared to create a setting in which to indulge the senses; from the moment you enter the door you feel wrapped in an aura of grandeur. If they are free, get the room with the *dossel*, a gorgeous four-poster bed with romantic drapes and gilded woodwork, or the blue room that hints of Venician decadence and *louche* desporting. Splendid original artworks fill the walls, many of them with a Moorish theme and though they may not be Old Masters, they give a feeling of permanence and style. The high ceilings and heavy, cream-washed furniture of the cafeteria make you feel as if you are waiting for the lord of the manor to return from the hunt; the splendid meat from the Basque country served in the restaurant tells you that he has arrived. The billiard room is not a place merely to knock a few balls about — national and European championships are held in a professionally laid-out arena. Even the weather vane is decorated with a chap playing the long cue.

What to see and do: Ibi toy museum, Font Roja natural park, Castalla castle.

POU DE LA NEU

MAP 04

Alt de la Carrasqueta s/n, Xixona
03100, Alicante

Tel: 667 531 023/667 428 263

e-mail: xixona@poudelaneu.com

Web Page: www.poudelaneu.com

Closed: July

Bedrooms: 3 Doubles, 4 Twins, all en suite

Prices: €80 including VAT

Meals: Breakfast included, Lunch/Dinner €20 including wine and VAT

Getting there: Take the N332 from Alicante in the direction of Valencia and just before el Campello take the N340 to Alcoy and Xixona. After Xixona continue the steep, twisting climb to Alcoy. Shortly after you pass a filling station and small housing estate on your left a sign indicates the Puerto de la Carrasqueta. Immediately after that a small sign points right to the Pou de la Neu, two kilometres up a cement road.

Management: Antonio Pérez

Pou de la Neu is the highest hotel and restaurant in Alicante province, and it is said that on a clear day you can see as far as Ibiza from its terraces. "Pou" refers to the ancient ice pit next to the hotel, where mountain snow was once densely packed to form ice for the making of ice cream in nearby Xixona. Completely refurbished in 2002, Pou de la Neu is owned by the local authority but Antonio, who leases it, couldn't be more proud of it than if he'd laid every stone himself. Unpretentious but elegant furnishings create an ambience in keeping with the tranquillity of the hotel's situation. Not a television in sight, but each room has a small stereo system, complete with CDs to lull the visitor into a state of repose. Herbs for Antonio's excellent kitchen are grown in the hotel's own garden (open to visitors) and used in the preparation of regional dishes with a twist. Deserts are based on the sweets, ice creams and *turrón* from Xixona, famous throughout Spain for its almond-based delicacies. Not the place for those in a rush because there's nothing to do here but wander the mountain paths or relax.

What to see and do: Xixona, home of *Turrón*, Ibi toy museum, Font Roja National Park.

EL SESTER

MAP 04

Calle Finestrat 2, Torremanzanas
03108, Alicante

Tel: 965 619 017

e-mail: elseber@arrakis.es

Web Page: www.hotelsester.com

Closed: Never

Bedrooms: 1 Single, 9 Doubles, 4 Twins

Prices: Single €55-59, Double/Twin €87-96 including VAT

Meals: Breakfast included, Lunch/Dinner €15 excluding drinks and VAT, but need to be ordered in advance on weekdays during winter

Getting there: From the N332 coastal road at Villajoyosa (La Vila Joiosa) follow the signs for the motorway but instead of joining it stay on the CV770 for Sella. Take the CV775 for Relleu before you reach Sella and continue around the edge of the village in the direction of Torremanzanas.

Management: María Llorens Giner

The *valenciano* phrase *"Menjar i Repós"* (eat and rest) is written across the top of El Sester's publicity material and María Lorens does everything she can to make sure that her hotel lives up to the ideal. Originally a 19th-century summer-house, the building underwent a complete renovation in 1998 to become a charming small hotel. Antiques are everywhere, but El Sester has a wonderful light and airy feeling, with spacious en-suite bedrooms, each one decorated differently in warm pastel colours, with rich fabrics and colonial-style furniture. A lift gives access to all floors. The restaurant, with its stone walls and flagged floor giving the feeling of a *bodega*, is well-respected throughout the area, serving traditional dishes, including local sausages and meats (you can buy some if you wish) and an inventive international cuisine. A brightly decorated bar/cafeteria brings an air of Mediterranean jollity, but if you want the real sandy thing the beach is only a 40-minute drive away. In May, Torremanzanas celebrates one of the strangest fiestas on the Costa Blanca, Pa Beneit, when young ladies wander the streets with enormous loaves of bread balanced precariously on their heads.

What to see and do: *Turrón* manufacturing at Xixona, Moors and Chris-tians museum at Alcoy, Font Roja national park.

LAS PUERTAS DEL INDIANO

MAP 05

Calle Alicante 23, Relleu
03578, Alicante

Tel: 966 856 326 / 605 253 188

e-mail: correo@puertasindiano.com

Web Page: www.puertasindiano.com

Closed: Never

Bedrooms: 2 Doubles, 4 Twins

Prices: €89-92 including VAT

Meals: Breakfast included, Dinner €18 excluding wine and VAT

Getting there: From the N332 coastal road at La Vila Joiosa follow the signs for the motorway but instead of joining it stay on the CV770 for Sella. Take the CV775 for Relleu before you reach Sella. It's best to park on the edge of the village. Las Puertas is in the town square next to the church.

Management: María Dolores González and Jorge Minguell

Few *casas rurales* hold the surprises behind their façades that you discover when you open the lustrous doors that give the name to this hotel — the doors are graced by two beautifully carved heads. Deep pink walls, beamed ceilings and graceful furniture set the scene of Edwardian elegance. But what appears to be the glass wall of a small patio is actually part of an ultra-modern spa. When beautician and masseuse María Dolores (call her Lola) and doctor Jorge fled Madrid for the peacefulness of the Alicante mountains, they converted a ruined townhouse into a refuge from stress and everyday life: no televisions, no smoking and no children. Visitors can just relax in the softly painted and cosily decorated bedrooms and comfortable lounge, dining in the tiny restaurant that serves healthy local recipes based on the Mediterranean diet. But it would be a pity not to make the most of the bubbling hydromassage or one of Lola's wonderful massages (if you've never tried a mud massage you've never lived!). Packages are available that include a wide range of beauty and therapeutic treatments, all undertaken in the hotel's professionally-equipped treatment room.

What to see and do: Nearby beaches, painted houses of La Vila Joiosa, Cuevas de Canelobre.

ALMASSERA VELLA

MAP 05

Carrer de la Mare de Deu del Miracle 56, Relleu
03578, Alicante

Tel: 966 856 003 **Fax:** 966 856 337

e-mail: oldolivepress@tiscali.es

Web Page: www.oldolivepress.com

Closed: Never

Bedrooms: 3 Doubles, 1 Twin, 1 Apartment. Five-bedroom cottage can be rented separately

Prices: €70 including breakfast. Variable rates for apartment and cottage

Meals: Dinner €17.50 to order

Getting there: Take exit 66 for Villajoyosa from A7 coastal motorway, heading towards Sella. After passing Orcheta take the left signed Relleu. In the village find main square in front of church. Take the street opposite the church door. Almassera is at the bottom of the street on right. Unload and park 50 metres further on.

Management: Christopher and Marisa North

When Christopher and Marisa bought this old olive press on the cusp of the millennium, it had been empty for almost a decade. As the tiny rooms were picturesque but impractical, the building was almost completely gutted to create a light and spacious interior with views across the rugged terrain opposite. They even bought the ruin on the opposite side of the valley so no-one could spoil the view. Christopher runs poetry and painting holidays so the house was designed to give space for study, with a large library and public areas that can be equally private. The house is beautifully decorated throughout and, from the plant-covered patio you can gaze to infinity across the swimming pool. Marisa provides the excellent cuisine, usually regional dishes with a fair smattering of traditional and adapted, that keeps their guests content. The bedrooms are small but comfortably furnished, probably working on the premise that the rest of the house is so comfortable that you won't want to spend much time in them anyway. A delightful, two-bedroom apartment in the cottage opposite the main house is fully-fitted for those who prefer privacy and the whole cottage can be rented for those wanting a longer stay.

What to see and do: The beaches of Villajoyosa, the Cuevas de Canelobre and walking in the mountains around Puig Campana.

EL ALMENDRAL

MAP 05

Ptda Rural El Terme, Relleu
03578, Alicante

Tel: 659 165 085

e-mail: info@almendral.com

Web Page: www.almendral.com

Closed: Never

Bedrooms: 5 Doubles, 2 Twins, 1 Apartment

Prices: Double/Twin €85-140, Apartment €190-220 including VAT

Meals: Breakfast included, Lunch/Dinner €18 guest menu excluding drinks

Getting there: Take the CV 775 from El Campello for Aigües, passing through the village in the direction of Relleu. After you see a large cream-coloured house on your right (Mas Blanch) the road dips to the left. At the bottom of the dip a sign to the left up a track indicates El Almendral.

Management: Bernard Vassas

If you're looking for a sinful hotel, look no further than El Almendral, because each of the sumptuous bedrooms are named and decorated in keeping with the seven deadly sins. You can choose "pride" in the violet room, "lust" in the blue one or revel in the "gluttony" of the orange. When ebullient Frenchman Bernard created El Almendral from little more than a small farmhouse, he brought not just his French chic but also exquisite furniture from his homes in Miami and Cuba. Luxuriant, deep leather sofas, enormous beds, gorgeous artworks and antiques all add an air of decadence in keeping with the sybaritic ambience of the hotel. Some of the rooms have private terraces that overlook the almond groves that give the hotel its name, and if you fancy something very special, the apartment even has a bedroom with its own jacuzzi in the room. The small restaurant, elegantly decorated with original 18th and 19th-century paintings, serves excellent international and regional cuisine, including local wild boar. Bernard can arrange the hire of a vintage Rolls, Ferrari or other classic car if the urge for opulence overwhelms you.

What to see and do: Guadalest mountain village, Cuevas de Canalobre, Xixona.

CASA SALLY

MAP 04

Ptda Pla Cabeçó, Sector 2, 16, Busot
03111, Alicante

Tel: 965 975248 / 606 893 828

Closed: Never

Bedrooms: 3 Doubles, 1 Apartment

Prices: Double €50, Apartment €60, including VAT

Meals: Full English breakfast included, Dinner €15, including wine, but must be booked in advance

Getting there: From Campello on the N332 take the CV777 (or CV773 from the N340 to Alcoy/Xixona) to Busot. Drive through the village in the direction of Xixona. As you leave Busot there are several named country roads on your right. Take the second road signed Cabeçó (it has a number 2 on it). Follow the road until you pass a breezeblock wall on your left. Casa Sally is the last house in a short row on the left.

Management: Sally and Keith Langsbury

Anyone travelling in Spain who's missing a bit of English cosiness need look no further than Casa Sally. For 10 years Sally and Keith had a small village house until they built Casa Sally at the foot of the Cabec d'Or mountain. Comfortable chairs, a big fire in winter and satellite television seem designed to lull you into a post-lunch doze, while in summer you can lounge by the pool or make yourself a barbecue in the open-air kitchen. But it's the welcome that's most important, and the couple make you feel as if you are sharing their home — as indeed you are. If they happen to be hosting one of their regular parties for Spanish friends, you will probably be invited to join in. At any other time make sure you sample Sally's cooking because she comes from a long line of chefs and is often booked to create special meals in private homes. Nothing is too much trouble: airport pick-ups, guided tours, beach runs and a wealth of local information to guide you on your way. There's even a washing machine, plus iron, for the use of guests.

What to see and do: Cuevas de Canelobre, Xixona for *turrón*, local beaches.

FINCA EL OTERO

MAP 04

Calle Atalaya 60, Aigües de Busot
03569, Alicante

Tel: 965 690 116

e-mail: info@finceloter.com

Web Page: www.fincaelotero.com

Closed: Christmas & New Year

Bedrooms: 1 Doubles, 3 Twins, all en suite

Prices: Double/Twin €65-85 including VAT

Meals: Breakfast included, Lunch/Dinner €12.50 excluding wine. A couple of good tapas bars in village 10 minutes walk away

Getting there: The CV775 from the N332 coastal road goes direct to Aigües. Drive into the village and just after a sharp left turn (beside La Taverna) a small sign for El Otero directs you to the left. Follow the twisting road up the hill. In front of a wall painted deep red there is a short track to the right that leads to El Otero's car park.

Management: Evelyn Kraft and Marie Dardenne

When Belgian sisters-in-law Evelyn and Marie moved to Spain with their respective husbands and children, they were inundated with visitors so decided to convert the ground-floor storerooms into four spacious en-suite bedrooms. Elegantly furnished and decorated (look closely at some of the paintings and views and you will realise that they are trompe l'oeil), each room has large French windows that open on to a sunny terrace with beautiful views across the valley and down to the sea. In summer visitors can take breakfast at their own table just outside their front door, but most people choose to join the other guests at a large communal table on the terrace. For breakfast you will be served jams and marmalades made in Evelyn and Marie's own kitchen. Each pair of bedrooms is linked and has a small separate dining area so they can be used individually or as family suites. While parents lounge around the circular swimming pool, the kids can have a whale of a time in the separate playground, built to keep the duo's own five children happy and now equally enjoyed by visitors. With mountains at hand for walking and golden beaches for lazing only 15 minutes away, visitors have the best of both worlds.

What to see and do: Guadalest mountain village, Villajoyosa old town, beaches.

FINCA MARBEUF

MAP 04

Partida Peñacerrada 17, Muchamel
03110, Alicante

Tel: 965 950 282 **Fax:** 965 950 612

e-mail: info@marbeuf.com

Web Page: www.marbeuf.com

Closed: Never

Bedrooms: 14 Doubles, 4 Apartments

Prices: €75-125 per room, including in apartments, excluding breakfast and VAT

Meals: All rooms/apartments have access to full catering facilities. Meals can be ordered in from a nearby restaurant and there are plenty of places to eat in the town

Getting there: From the N332 coastal road near Campello take the road signposted Valencia and Madrid N340/A31 (also signposted for the airport). Stay on the road that goes over the motorway following signs for Xixona and Muchamel. Pass the first Muchamel sign (for *centro ciudad*). Take a left at the next Muchamel sign (also for Sant Juan de Alacant) and go right at the first roundabout. Stay on this road until you pass between two filling stations and enter Muchamel. Take the right to Tangel and moments later right again by the Restaurant Venteta. The hotel is 200 metres on the right

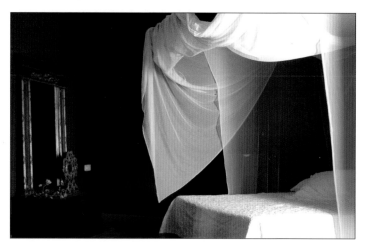

Management: Helen van der Zee

Some hotels have the "wow" factor, but few of them to the same degree as the Marbeuf. Walk through the ancient wooden doors into the 300-year-old nobleman's house and feel yourself step back in time to a grandeur that these days most of us only see in Hollywood movies. Museum-quality antiques and art works are everywhere (the sandstone statue of the lady next to the *bodega* was originally at Versailles, before she was replaced by a marble copy) and the layout of the hotel means that you can enjoy the privacy of your own room or share a stunning apartment, heavy with to-die-for antiques and painted frescos. The apartments are the height of luxury, each with its own idiosyncratic style. They have fully-equipped kitchens but, for anyone who wants restaurant dining without moving outside the building, meals can be delivered from the nearby Venteta restaurant. The 12,000-square-metre gardens are planted with palm, lemon, orange, almond and olive trees and grapevines, with lawns surrounding the swimming pool and gazebos to provide shade from the summer sun. Marbeuf even has its own chapel, still used for the occasional wedding.

What to see and do: Castillo de Santa Barbara in Alicante, Xixona for *turrón*, Cuevas de Canalobras in Busot.

HARTENDALE

MAP 06

Partida Purgateros 5, Encebras
03650, Alicante

Tel: 965 878 012

Closed: Never

Bedrooms: 3 Doubles, 1 Twin

Prices: Double €36-40, Twin €36 including VAT and breakfast

Meals: Packed lunch €5, Dinner €15 to order

Getting there: On the N330 Alicante-Madrid road take the turning after Novelda for Loma Bada. As the slip road rises, go left to a bridge over the motorway. At next roundabout follow the road for Pinoso/El Pino. Just before you get there, look for the antique shop Rusta Originals on a slight rise to the left and take the next left for Encebras. Continue through Encebras, staying on the narrow road without deviating. When you see the sign for Purgateros, you will see a group of houses to the right. Take the track that appears to go into a field but leads to the hamlet.

Management: Brian and Biddy Baggott

The name alone confirms that this delightful little *casa rural* is English-run. (The name comes from the farm where Biddy grew up.) Far from ending up in purgatory as the hamlet's name might suggest, the few houses that sit together are set amid peace and tranquillity. There are long views over vineyards and you can enjoy walks in the national park behind. From their bi-annual forays to the UK the couple bring back paint and fabrics, testament to Biddy's belief that for some things the British can't be beaten. Her discerning eye and colour use have created a lovely, restful home with soft hues enlivened by vivid splashes of colour and plenty of room to spread out. Guests have their own lounge but most prefer to sit and chat with Brian and Biddy, especially during the winter months, warmed by the splendid wood-burning stove. The area is one of the main wine-growing regions in Alicante province and there are plenty of *bodegas* to visit as well as a wine route to follow. If a museum visit is a must, Elda has the weirdly wonderful shoe museum, the only one of its kind in Spain.

What to see and do: Spa at Fortuna, local bodegas, shoe museum at Elda.

HOSPEDERÍA EL BATÁN

MAP 07

Ctra Comarcal 1512 km 43, Tramacastilla
44112, Teruel

Tel: 978 706 070

Web Page: www.elbatan.net

Closed: Never

Bedrooms: 3 Doubles, 5 Twins, 1 four-bed Apartment

Prices: Double/Twin €60, Apartment €104 including VAT

Meals: Breakfast €6, Lunch/Dinner €25-30, residents'menu €20 including wine, *menú degustación* €30 excluding wine

Getting there: After Teruel on the N234 from Valencia continue through Albarracín. Shortly after Torres de Albarracín, at km 43 marker a small sign to the left directs you to the hotel, which you see among the trees.

Management: Sebastián Roselló and María José Meda

El Batán looks as if it has existed since Noah was a lad, but the building is only seven years old, constructed by one of the local training schools where artisans learn their skills on top-notch projects. All the elements of traditional regional construction are there, even to the restoration of the mill-race that drove the original waterwheel — a woollen mill stood on the site for centuries. The Hospedería has that difficult-to-attain combination of cosiness and elegance. The rich colours of the walls contrast with muted upholstery fabrics. Smart sabre-backed mahogany chairs grace the dining room, chunky country pine the public rooms and the uncluttered bedrooms are tastefully furnished with antiques. The hotel is popular, especially at weekends, but the restaurant — said to be one of the top three in Teruel province — is the star attraction. The *menú degustación*, a sampling of some of the best dishes, is a salivating delight; its various sections bear such titles as *"Fino, Suave"* (Fine, Smooth), *"Intenso, Silvestre"* (Intense, Wild) and *"Ternura, Potencia"* (Tenderness, Power). A wonderful place to sample the best of Spanish food in idyllic surroundings without the drive home.

What to see and do: Albarracín historic village, the Ruta del Agua, Pranceres castle.

CASONA DEL AJÍMEZ

MAP 07

San Juan 2, Albarracín
44100, Teruel

Tel: 978 710 321 / 655 843 207

e-mail: c.ajimez@arrakis.es

Web Page: www.casonadelajimez.arrakis.es

Closed: Never

Bedrooms: 6 Doubles

Prices: €72 excluding 7% VAT

Meals: Breakfast €4.50, Lunch/Dinner €25-30 excluding wine (dinner only during the week)

Getting there: Just after Teruel on the N234 from Valencia, take the A1512 to Albarracín. In the town take the cobbled street that goes up to the left at the entrance to the road tunnel. Follow the zig-zagging street until you come to a car park. Leave the car here and take the street, San Juan, leading away from the car park. The hotel is on the left almost at the end of the street.

Management: Javier Lahuerta

When Mickey Mouse ran around medieval streets in *The Sorcerer's Apprentice,* Walt Disney must have been inspired by Albarracín, a mountain-top village with streets so narrow that neighbours can not only shake hands from their windows but probably share the same curtains. You could imagine Walt designing the Casona del Ajímez, but that singular honour goes to owner Javier. Describe the hotel as gaudy, over-the-top, kitsch, whatever and you would be absolutely right – and that's its charm. There are only six bedrooms, two inspired by the Christian faith, two by the Jewish and two by the Muslim, although without an explanation you may find it difficult to differentiate. One even has a window in the bed head and another incorporates a *menorah*, the seven-branched Jewish candelabra, incorporated into a four-poster bed. The comfortable dining room sports a large library table on which, at first sight, illuminated medieval music scripts are laid out for your perusal, but which turn out to be pretty nifty paint jobs. Despite or because of the whimsy, Casona del Ajimez is a delightful hotel, and if the weather is fine you can take breakfast in the garden below the walls of the 10th-century castle. Vegetarian food is available to order.

What to see and do: The whole village of Albarracín is a National Monument, the neolithic rock paintings in the Pinares de Rodeno nature park, Peracense castle.

CASA DE SANTIAGO

MAP 07

Subida de las Torres 11, Albarracín
44100, Teruel

Tel: 978 700 316 **Fax:** 978 710 141

Web Page: www.casadesantiago.net

Closed: Never

Bedrooms: 4 Doubles, 5 Twins

Prices: €58-64 including VAT

Meals: Breakfast €6, Lunch €18, Dinner €20-25, both including wine

Getting there: Just after Teruel on the N234 from Valencia, take the A1512 to Albarracín. In the town take the cobbled street up to the left at the entrance to the road tunnel. Make your way to the Plaza Mayor and park (it's best to ask directions when you get there because the streets are a warren). Take the steps up from the plaza and the hotel is on the right, opposite the church.

Management: María Jesús Sorian

This hotel demonstrates that three centuries ago not all priests were as poor as church mice — it is practically a *palacio*. One of the oldest houses in the village, it was the home of the priest who tended the flock of the Iglesia de Santiago, a few steps across the narrow cobbled street. María Jesús has what could be described as an eclectic taste when it comes to colour schemes. Waking up in a four-poster bed draped with lush purple hangings in a bedroom decorated in lime green, orange, yellow and pale blue may sound like a Technicolor nightmare, but it works and works beautifully. The hotel is full of "ooh" and "aah" decorative features, from the orange-walled sitting room with its comfortable sofas, to the gorgeous, yellow and pale blue sun room at the top of the house, with stunning views from its big picture windows over the village rooftops to the mountain beyond. The popular restaurant, rather more reserved in its décor, serves typical Aragonese dishes, including the delicious *ternasco*, a special breed of lamb, particular to the region — it bears the *Denominación de Origen de Aragón* label.

What to see and do: Albarracín village, walks in the Sierra de Albarracín, Pinares de Rodeno Nature Park.

HOSPEDERÍA EL ZORZAL

MAP 07

Calle El Horno 27, Valdecuenca
44122, Teruel

Tel: 978 788 121 **Fax:** 978 788 195

Web Page: www.elzorzal.net

Closed: Never

Bedrooms: 6 Doubles

Prices: €45-50 exluding VAT

Meals: Breakfast €4.50, Lunch €15 including wine, Dinner €25-30, *menú degustación* €22.50 both excluding wine

Getting there: N234 from Valencia by-passing Teruel. Just after Teruel take the A1513 to San Blas, continuing past Bezas. As you enter Valdecuenca (a tiny village) there are signs to the hotel.

Management: Carlos Soriano Lozano

Since it was built as a nobleman's house in the 16th century, little has changed structurally at El Zorzal until it was restored to become a hotel in 2002, although minor alterations were made when it was a wayside lodging house and a village shop. The house was restored by the Albarracín municipal council, one of its projects to convert run-down historic houses into country hotels — and an excellent job it is doing. The hotel looks tiny as you enter the front door but expands rapidly once inside. Low ceilings and great oak beams take you back to Dickensian times and you half expect a buxom serving wench to stroll by with tankards of foaming ale. Instead, you get the quiet formality of Carlos who escorts you to one of the charming rooms, some of which are directly under the eaves. You are miles from anywhere, in a village where a sauntering cat is the rush hour, but the elegant restaurant brings diners from far and wide to sample excellent regional cuisine. You may even be offered *zorzal (*thrush*)* — everything is eaten, even the bones.

What to see and do: Albarracín medieval village, Roderno nature park, neolithic paintings.

CASA DEL IRLANDÉS

MAP 08

Calle Virgen del Carmen 18, Rubielos de Mora
44415, Teruel

Tel: 978 804 462 / 649 612 635

e-mail: casairlandes@ya.com

Web Page: www.casadelirlandes.com

Closed: Never

Bedrooms: 4 Double, 1 Quadruple all en-suite. Extra beds available

Prices: Double €38 including VAT

Meals: Breakfast €3.50. No other meals provided but plenty of excellent restaurants in the village

Getting there: Take the N234 from Valencia to Teruel, turning on to the A1515 at Venta del Aire beside what looks like a motorway service station. As you enter the village, moments after a Y-junction with the road from Mora de Rubielos, take the first right. You enter a small plaza with Casa Mata, a butcher, in front of you. Keep to the right following the street to a small font on the left, where you take a left up a narrow street, then left again. The house is on the left.

Management: David and Sylvia Maddock

Rubielos de Mora may not be as famous as its near neighbour Albarracín, but it is arguably as pretty and intriguing, with narrow medieval streets and stout civic/ecclesiastic architecture. Many of the houses are almost Tyrolean in their appearance, with their overhanging roofs and wooden balconies, and in one of these Sylvia (Spanish) and David (Irish) have created their delightful small hotel, incorporating the style and hospitality of the two nationalities. The rooms are cosy and colourful with lots of light, mainly furnished in pine and with beautiful Irish dressers, a reminder of their years in Ireland. If David takes a liking to you, and he seems to take a liking to everyone, he may invite you into his glory hole, a wonderful, kitschy little bar full of Irish memorabilia — the perfect place for the "*craic*". Staying at Casa del Irlandés is almost like having a couple of days with pals because the couple not only go out of their way to make your stay an enjoyable one, but have extensive knowledge of the area and the best things to see.

What to see and do: The whole of the historic village, Mudejar Teruel, Dianopolis dinosaur world.

HOTEL DE LA VILLA

MAP 08

Plaza Carmen 2, Rubielos de Mora
44415, Teruel

Tel: 968 804 640 **Fax:** 978 804 514

e-mail: hoteldelavilla@sierradegudar.com

Web Page: www.hotel-de-la-villa.com

Closed: Never

Bedrooms: 7 Doubles, 7 Twins, 1 Suite, all en suite

Prices: Double/Twin €75, Suite €150, including VAT

Meals: Breakfast €6, Lunch €18 including wine, Dinner €30

Getting there: Take the N234 from Valencia to Teruel, turning on to the A1515 at Venta del Aire beside what looks like a motorway service station. As you pass through Rubielos, you see a long wall on your right with a narrow arch in it (Portal del Carmen). Pass through the arch and the hotel is in the plaza directly in front of you.

Management: Angel Esplez Soriano

This building goes back to the 15th century, when it was built by a noble family from Valencia. Since then it has acquired various architectural embellishments, including some grand 19th-century Gothic features. By the time Angel Esplez bought it in 2001 it was in a bit of a shambles and he spent the next two years restoring it from top to bottom, maintaining the original fabric wherever possible. The theme is set by the grand entrance hall, with its flagged floor, wood-panelled ceiling and huge, Gothic stone arch. For lovers of the keyboard there's a fine Victorian organ in one corner. The stately staircase takes you to simply but elegantly furnished bedrooms. If you are in a splash-out mood, go for the suite with its *dossel*, a four-poster bed with drapes. The locality is one of the most important in Europe for black truffles and the outrageously priced fungus is used – sparingly – in the traditional cuisine provided by the hotel's kitchen. You could also try *carne de caza mayor*, basically large wild animals including wild boar and deer. During the warmth of summer the garden acts as an extension to the restaurant.

What to see and do: Medieval Rubielos, ski slopes at Valdelinares, walking in the surrounding hills.

HOTEL LOS LEONES

MAP 08

Plaza Igual y Gil 3, Rubielos de Mora
44415, Teruel

Tel: 978 804 477

e-mail: hoteleones@sierradegudar.com

Web Page: www.losleones.info

Closed: Never

Bedrooms: 10 Doubles, 2 Twins

Prices: €80 including VAT

Meals: Breakfast €6, Lunch €20 including wine, Dinner €22-25 excluding wine. During winter months it is necessary to book a meal during the week. Vegetarian food to order

Getting there: Take the N234 from Valencia to Teruel, turning on to the A1515 at Venta del Aire beside what looks like a motorway service station. As you pass through Rubielos, you see a long wall on your right with a narrow arch in it (Portal del Carmen). Pass through the arch and down the right side of the Hotel de la Villa into the next square. The hotel is on the right.

Management: Pilar Torán Lorenz and Manuel Górriz Martín

The corrugated plasterwork (*revoltones*) you see on the outside of the hotel and a couple of other grand houses in the village is not a regional architectural feature but an attempt to stop the village lads practising *pelot*, the local handball game, on the large expanse of wall and leaving ball marks on it. This architectural feature has been there since the 19th century and, when Pilar and Manuel restored this noble structure, they wisely decided to leave them there. No-one knows who built the original house, but in latter years it was the village bar, local shop, *casino* (businessmen's club), and the local dancehall — a number of elderly village ladies remember performing the *pasodoble* there with their boyfriends. The couple have done a superb restoration, and every corner is a colourful delight to the eye. Antiques fill the rooms but are there to be enjoyed and not fretted over. Even after six years of running the hotel, Pilar's delight in her home is still obvious. She'll happily show you around and bring out the photo album to show how much they had to do to create their lovely hotel.

What to see and do: Medieval Rubielos, Mudejar architecture in Teruel, local mountain walks.

HOSPEDERÍA MOLINO DE SABAJOSA

MAP 09

Ctra. Cehegín-Calasparra, Valentín
30420, Murcia

Tel: 968 720 170 **Fax:** 968 433 087

e-mail: sahajosa@wanadoo.es

Web Page: www.molinosahajosa.com

Closed: Never

Bedrooms: 6 Doubles, 4 Twins

Prices: €48 plus 7% VAT. Single person €36. Includes breakfast

Meals: No meals are provided but the village has a restaurant and two *tapas* bars

Getting there: From the C415 Murcia-Caravaca de la Cruz take the C3314 just afte Cehegín in the direction of Calasparra. After about 10 km take the right turn for Valentín. Take a left at the T-junction and right when you see a sign for the Molino. The short road ends in the Molino's car park.

Management: Belén López

Don't be put off as you drive into the courtyard if the Molino appears a bit worn around the edges – you are about to enter a curious place where barely a stick of furniture has changed since the early 1900s. Unintentionally, it charts a family's decorative taste since the flour mill started in 1786. The original equipment used for separating the wheat almost fills the entrance and almost all the remaining space is cluttered with art objects. Belén's father, Vicente, could have been politely called a magpie and his collection of just about anything and everything fills the first floor: ancient agricultural instruments, post cards, gramophones, a posse of miniature bullfighters, pots, pans, radios, the weird and wonderful that any number of museums would give their eye teeth for. A couple of bedrooms are also furnished with family heirlooms. Look over the balcony and you'll see the great grindstones and belt-flapping, Heath Robinson-like machinery that kept the mill going. But not all is ancient; a huge swimming pool is just the place to while away the summer hours or you can take a glass of something in the shade of the vines.

What to see and do: Caravaca del la Cruz (designated a religious city) with 'White' and 'Blue' fiesta museums, Santuario de la Esperanze in Calasparra.

CASA DEL CASCO VIEJO

MAP 09

Calle la Tria 15, Cehegín
30430, Murcia

Tel: 96 874 2007 / 667 563 397

e-mail: casadelcascoviejo@fastmail.fm

Web Page: www.casadelcascoviejo.com

Closed: Never

Bedrooms: 3 Suites sleeping 2-6

Prices: €25 per person, minimum stay 2 nights, including breakfast and VAT

Meals: Lunch to order €20 including wine. Plenty of restaurant and *tapas* bars in the town

Getting there: From Murcia take the E15(N340) in the direction of Granada and Almería. After approximately 8 km take the exit C415 to Mula. Continue to Cehegín, taking exit 55 (oeste). Turn right at first and second roundabouts. At third roundabout (with a fountain and statue of shoemaker) turn right on Gran Via. Take 3rd left, right at crossroads and immediately left into Calle Vera Cruz. Follow the road as it bears right. The Casco Viejo is the blue house on the left.

Management: Sean and Suzanne Roberts

Suzanne and Sean are a perfect example of a couple who do their utmost to make life in Spain a success and to ensure everyone who stays with them has a jolly good time. The accommodation consists of three suites, each pleasingly furnished in modern rustic style where clients can relax with the wine provided on arrival. The comfortable house and warm welcome are only part of what visitors can expect. If you need a pampering hairdo, Susanne has a salon in the town and, if you need information about what to do, Sean can tell you because he runs a local magazine that keeps the local British community up to date with what's going on in the area. He might even invite you on to his radio programme. If you want an activity holiday, you can try walking or painting classes, but if you'd like to feel part of the rural community at harvest time you can spend a day picking olives and almonds and take the produce home with you. The area is a major wine producer and you can complete your gastronomic break by sampling wines at the local *bodegas*.

What to see and do: Caravaca holy city, Murcia, *bodegas* tour.

MOLINO DEL RÍO

MAP 09

Camino Viejo de Archivel s/n, Caravaca de la Cruz
30400, Murcia

Tel: 968 433 381 / 606 301 409 **Fax:** 968 433 444

e-mail: elmolino@molinodelrio.com

Web Page: www.molinodelrio.com

Closed: Never

Bedrooms: 1 Double, 6 Apartments sleeping 2-6

Prices: Double €55 (€30 single usage), Apartments €82-96 including breakfast, excluding VAT

Meals: Lunch/Dinner €15-18 including wine

Getting there: Leave Caravaca de la Cruz on the C330 following the signs for Andalucía. You will see a sign for the Molino after 4 km at the right turn for Benablón. Follow the signs until you arrive in the Molino's car park.

Management: Carmen Alvarez and Jan Hallmér

As a final dramatic view presents itself, the road drops into what looks like the car park of a small house except that this one extends into a series of small plazas that create a village feel. The building began life in the early 1500s as a flour mill, the oldest recorded one in the area. Barely a sound disturbs the peace other than the twittering of birds and the tinkling of the fountain in the cobbled courtyard. The original structure of the mill remains unchanged, including some of the stone floors said to come from an original Roman mill on the site. Most of the rooms are self-catering apartments with a small kitchen area, but you're not obliged to cook as local produce, home-grown where possible, features on the menu. International dishes and Scandinavian cuisine reflect Jan's Swedish roots. A short walk through the garden, scented by the lavender beds, brings you to a large swimming pool fed by the estate's natural springs. During summer months a delightful outdoor dining room with a great barbecue is the place to while away an evening. From early 2006 a spa offering a range of therapies is to be added.

What to see and do: Caravaca holy city, wine museum and *bodegas* in Bullas, Mula thermal baths.

HOSPEDERÍA EL MOLINO DE FELIPE

MAP 09

Ribera de los Molinos 321, Mula
30170, Murcia

Tel: 968 662 013 or 607 754 477 **Fax:** 968 662 013

e-mail: molinofelipe@paralelo40.org

Web Page: www.parelelo40.org/molinofilipe

Closed: Never

Bedrooms: 6 Doubles, 4 Twins, 3 Apartments

Prices: Double/Twin €48 (€28 single use) including VAT and breakfast,
Apartment €72-100 including VAT but excluding breakfast

Meals: Lunch €9, Dinner €12 plus VAT to order

Getting there: C415 Autopista from Murcia taking exit for Mula and
Pliego (not Mula Pueblo or Baños de Mula). Bypass Mula in the direction
Bullas. Three km from Mula, as you enter El Niño, take the small road
to the side of Casa de Paco. One km further is a sign for the Molino.
Follow this to the entrance gates of an ochre building. Turn right into the
car park of a pale salmon-coloured building opposite.

Management: Felipe Sánchez Ruiz

If you've an interest in how bread was made in the good old days, here's the place to gain an insight. Next to the hotel operates one of Spain's few still-functioning, old-style flour mills. It supplies quality, totally natural flour, to shops throughout the country – you can buy some yourself. The original mill dates from the 16th century, although the equipment used today is a little more modern, dating from the early 1900s. However, the hotel is absolutely up-to-date, even having a gymnasium for those who don't want to just lounge around the pool. The rooms are light and welcoming, but you probably won't want to spend too much time in them, given the wonderful countryside surrounding the Hospedería. Passing by is part of the national Vía Verde network. This consists of old train and shepherd's tracks converted to cycling and walking routes. If you don't have a bike with you, you can hire one. Meals are to order and, where possible, produce grown in the Molino's own gardens is used. Breakfast can be taken on the long veranda with 45-kilometre views across fruit groves.

What to see and do: Museo Arte Ibérico and 17th-century castle in Mula, the Roman and Moorish Molinos de Mula.

MOLINO DE ABAJO

MAP 09

Parega Molino de Abajo, Bullas
30180, Murcia

Tel: 968 431 383 / 609 672 784 **Fax:** 968 655 090

e-mail: turismo_rural@castillico.com

Web Page: www.castillo.com

Closed: Mondays

Bedrooms: 4 Doubles, 2 Twins, 3 Apartments, 2 Wood cabins to sleep 5

Prices: Double/Twin €55 including breakfast, Apartment €120 (minimum stay 2 persons for two nights, Cabins €160-200 (minimum stay 2 nights) all including VAT

Meals: Lunch/dinner €24-30 including wine and VAT

Getting there: Leave the C415 Murcia-Caravaca road at Bullas, heading towards Totana. As you leave Bullas, at a junction with a right-hand bend, a small sign for the Molino directs you straight ahead. You soon see another sign for the Molino with three flags above it (the bottom of the sign is obscured by a crash barrier). The road leads to the Molino car park.

Management: Martín Gea

If you like the sound of water to lull you to sleep, the Molino de Abajo is for you because a river runs right alongside it. As its name suggests, it was once a flour mill, going back 350 years. It is set in a small, secluded canyon, where birdsong and the tinkling of the river provide a musical accompaniment. A recent conversion has kept much of the structure intact, including a floor of cobbled stones and some of the old milling equipment. The bedrooms, in a modern wing, are comfortably furnished and spacious, while the cabins are set slightly apart from the main building. A 15-minute walk along a country path takes you to large lawns and the splendid swimming pools, one each for adults and children. The apartments are in a delightful *casita* next to the swimming pools. A small sports complex with a cafeteria is currently under construction and will be open in 2006. The hotel includes a popular restaurant.

What to see and do: Salto de Usero waterfall, wine museum and *bodegas* of Bullas, Ruta del Vino.

HOTEL NAME	TOWN	Nº IN BOOK
Alojamiento Turistíco La Villa	Requena	017
Almassera Vella	Relleu	063
Blanc Casa	Lliber	049
Ca Ferminet	Benisilli	027
Casa Anna	Chodos	005
Casa Carrascal	Parcent	043
Casa Cortina	Bugarra	014
Casa de la Costera	Artana	009
Casa de Santiago Albarracín	Albarracín	071
Casa del Casco Viego	Cehegin	077
Casa del Irlandés	Rubielos de Mora	073
Casa del Maco	Calpe	051
Casa del Pinar	Venta del Moro	020
Casa Doña Anita	San Antonio de Requena	016
Casa Folch	Castellfort	004
Casa Gallinera	Benissivà	031
Casa Louise	Pego	032
Casa Pilar	Castel de Castelles	046
Casa Rosa	Alcalali	044
Casa Rural El Canto	Campell	040
Casa Rural El Castellot	Alpatró	028
Casa Rural El Chato Chico	Beniaya	037
Casa Rural El Pinet	Alfafara	034
Casa Rural La Carrasca	Alpatró	029
Casa Rural La Casota	Fleix	038
Casa Rural La Parrá	Alpatró	030
Casa Rural Serrella	Balones	045
Casa Rural Teranova	Fleix	039
Casa Sally	Busot	065
Casa Serena	Chulilla	013
Caserío de Mirador	Jalon	052
Casona del Ajimez	Albarracín	070

HOTEL NAME	TOWN	Nº IN BOOK

HOTEL NAME	TOWN	Nº IN BOOK
Hotel Moli de Canyisset	Font d'En Caros	024
Hotel Mont Sant	Xàtiva	021
Hotel Rural Els Frares	Quatretondeta	047
La Casa Vieja	Rugat	023
Las Puertas del Indiano	Relleu	062
Los Dos Tilos	Biar	058
Mas de Madalena	Lucena del Cid	007
Mas de Pau	Penaguila	053
Mas Fontanelles	Bihar	056
Masia San Joaquín	Agres	035
Massia Ferrer	Segorbe	011
Molino de Abajo	Bullas	080
Molino del Río	Caravaca de la Cruz	078
Pou de la Neu	Xixona	060
Pueblo Jardín	Benimeli	034
Torre de Arriba	Benimantell	054

TOWN	HOTEL NAME	NO. IN BOOK
Albaida	El Panset	025
Albarracín	Casona del Ajimez	070
Albarracín	Casa de Santiago	071
Agres	Masia San Joaquín	035
Aigúes	Finca El Otero	066
Alcalali	Casa Rosa	044
Algimia d'Alfara	El Secanet	012
Alfafara	Casa Rural El Pinet	034
Alpatró	Casa Rural El Castellot	028
Alpatró	Casa Rural La Carrasca	029
Alpatró	Casa Rural La Parrá	030
Artana	Casa de la Costera	009
Balones	Casa Rural Serrella	045
Beniaya	Casa Rural El Chato Chico	037
Benimantell	Torre de Arriba	054
Benimarfull	Hostería Els Banys	036
Benimeli	Pueblo Jardín	034
Benisilli	Ca Ferminet	027
Benissa	Hotel Cases de Sant Jaume	050
Benissivà	Casa Gallinera	031
Biar	Finca Fanecaes	057
Biar	Los Dos Tilos	058
Biar	Mas Fontanelles	056
Bocairent	Hotel L'Estacio	041
Bocairent	Hotel L'Agora	042
Bugarra	Casa Cortina	014
Bullas	Molino de Abajo	080
Busot	Casa Sally	065
Cabanes	Hotel L'Aldaba	006
Calpe	Casa del Maco	051
Callosa d'En Sarriá	El Repos de Viatger	055
Campell	Casa Rural El Canto	040

TOWN	HOTEL NAME	NO. IN BOOK
Rubielos de Mora	Hotel Los Leones	075
Rugat	La Casa Vieja	023
Salem	Granja San Miguel	026
San Antonio de Requena	Casa Doña Anita	016
Segorbe	Hospederia El Palen	010
Segorbe	Massia Ferrer	011
Tárbena	Hotel de Tárbena	048
Torremanzanas	El Sester	061
Tramacastilla	Hospederia El Batan	069
Valdecuenca	Hospederia El Zorzal	072
Valentin	Hospederia Molino Sahajosa	076
Venta del Moro	Casa del Pinar	020
Vilafamés	El Jardín Vertical	008
Xàtiva	Hotel Mont Sant	021
Xàtiva	Hotel H. de la Virgen de las Nieves	022
Xixona	Pou de la Neu	060

YOUR OPINIONS

Please let us know about your experiences at the places that we include in this book. And please let us know about any good places that you discover which aren't included in this book.

NAME of HOTEL: _____

Date of visit: _____

Your comments: _____

_____

_____

Your opinion of the food & wine: _____

_____

_____

Your name: _____

Address: _____

_____

_____

Contact number: _____
(if you are happy to give us these details).

Please send by post to
       Derek Workman
       Calle Almirante Cadarso, 30-1
       46005 Valencia
       or by e-mail to derek@derekworkman-journalist.com
       (or from my web page www.derekworkman-journalist.com)

Many thanks